wildlands

of the Upper South

wildlands

of the Upper South

By John M. Thompson
Photographs by Raymond Gehman

NATIONAL GEOGRAPHIC
WASHINGTON, D.C.

Jefferson National Forest cloaks the Alleghenies in southwestern Virginia.
Page one: An overgrown trail in the Monongahela National Forest beckons
hikers to explore. Pages 2-3: A monarch butterfly rests upon a blazing star

wildlands of the Upper South

Akron
Canton
Massillon
Butler
Aliquippa
State College
NEW YORK
N.Y.
PITTSBURGH
Johnstown
Altoona
Bethlehem
PENNSYLVANIA
Harrisburg
Reading
Trenton
Carlisle
Chambersburg
Gettysburg
York
Lancaster
Valley Forge
NEW JERSEY
Washington
Uniontown
PHILADELPHIA
Morgantown
Cumberland
Hagerstown
Frederick
Elkton
New Castle
Vineland
Cambridge
Wheeling
Fairmont
Grafton
MARYLAND
Winchester
Rock Creek Park
BALTIMORE
Dover
Bridgeton
Atlantic City
Marietta
Clarksburg
APPALACHIAN N.S.T.
Great Falls Park
Annapolis
Delaware Bay
Cape May
Athens
Parkersburg
Blackwater Falls S.P.
N.W.R.
Canaan Valley
Front Royal
Roosevelt Island
WASHINGTON
Alexandria
DELAWARE
Rehoboth Beach
Pint Pleasant
Cranesville Swamp
Elkins
GEORGE
SHENANDOAH NATIONAL PARK
Mason Neck S.P.
Cambridge
Ocean City
WEST VIRGINIA
MONONGAHELA
WASHINGTON
Prince William Forest Park
Salisbury
ASSATEAGUE ISLAND NATIONAL SEASHORE
Charleston
NATIONAL FOREST
Cranberry Glades Botanical Area
Watoga S.P.
NAT.
Ramsey's Draft Wilderness Area
Culpeper
Lexington Park
Chincoteague Bay
Gauley River N.R.A.
Babcock S.P.
Douthat S.P.
FOREST
Staunton
Charlottesville
Fredericksburg
Potomac
Chesapeake Bay
Chincoteague N.W.R.
Wallops Island
NEW RIVER GORGE NATIONAL RIVER
White Sulphur Springs
Lexington
VIRGINIA
Accomac
Beckley
James River S.P.
James
Richmond
Williamsburg
York
Cape Charles
Princeton
Mountain Lake Wilderness
Lynchburg
Appomattox
Petersburg
Yorktown
Kiptopeke S.P.
Bluefield
Roanoke
Blue Ridge Parkway
Hampton
Hampton Roads
JEFFERSON
NATIONAL FOREST
Pulaski
Radford
Newport News
Norfolk
Virginia Beach
Marion
Buffalo Mountain Natural Area Preserve
Martinsville
John H. Kerr Reservoir
Great Dismal Swamp N.W.R.
Portsmouth
Back Bay N.W.R.
MOUNT ROGERS N.R.A.
Danville
Elizabeth City
Grayson Highlands S.P.
Roanoke Rapids
Merchants Millpond S.P.
Bristol
Pilot Mountain S.P.
Hanging Rock S.P.
Reidsville
Henderson
Halifax
Kitty Hawk
Roan Mountain S.P.
PISGAH
Greensboro
Burlington
Edenton
Albemarle Sound
Jockey's Ridge S.P.
Winston-Salem
Eno River S.P.
Nags Head Woods Preserve
High Point
Chapel Hill
Durham
Rocky Mount
Manteo
Mount Mitchell S.P.
Lexington
Raleigh
Wilson
Greenville
Pea Island N.W.R.
FOREST
Hickory
Statesville
NORTH CAROLINA
Washington
CAPE HATTERAS
Mount Rogers
Kannapolis
Concord
Sanford
Goldsboro
Kinston
Cape Hatteras
NATIONAL SEASHORE
Gastonia
Charlotte
Albemarle
Raven Rock S.P.
Pamlico Sound
Ocracoke Inlet
Pinehurst
New Bern
Rock Hill
Monroe
Hamlet
Fayetteville
Spartanburg
Lancaster
Laurinburg
Jacksonville
Morehead City
CAPE LOOKOUT NATIONAL SEASHORE
Laurens
Wateree Lake
Lumberton
Cape Lookout
New River Inlet
Greenwood
Darlington
Marion
Whiteville
Wilmington
L. Murray
SOUTH CAROLINA
Florence
Lake Waccamaw S.P.
Columbia
Sumter
Conway
Southport
Cape Fear
Aiken
Orangeburg
Georgetown
Myrtle Beach
Augusta
Danmark
Summerville
Cape Romain
Bulls Bay
Walterboro
Estill
Charleston
Beaufort
Statesboro

Selected Features
National Park system
National Forest
National Wildlife Refuge
State Park, State Resort Park, State Nature Preserve, Natural Area Preserve
Other point of interest

introduction

Autumn spreads across the Upper South in two waves. It starts in the highlands of the Alleghenies, the Blue Ridge, and the Unakas: In mid-September a few maple and oak leaves turn prematurely yellow or crimson. Then the aspens and birches sense the change in season and take on a gold cast; the dogwoods begin turning a deep red, the sassafras a burnt orange. A wave of color spreads down the mountainsides to the east and west, painting the lower elevations. At the same time, in a second wave, fall marches from north to south. It may be November before the leaves turn in southeastern North Carolina and southwestern Tennessee. In spring, the reverse occurs—two great waves of blossoms head north and to the highlands. Early-blooming redbud, dogwood, and serviceberry test the spring air at low elevations; it may be two months from the time the first trilliums and mayapples emerge in the lowlands to the time they appear in the mountains. Similarly, brilliant flame azaleas begin flowering in late April in the Piedmont, but the time to see them in the Smokies is late June or even early July.

In brilliant fall foliage, a highbush blueberry shrub crowns a boulder in West Virginia's Dolly Sods Wilderness, an area of high windswept bogs and plains.

Each season brings a distinct personality, a rich profusion of colors and scents and sounds, to each wild corner of the Upper South—from the coast to the mountains and beyond. More temperate than the Deep South but no less lavish in its beauty, the Upper South prizes its abundant wildlands, its bird-frequented shores, stream-etched woodlands, and misty blue mountains. This varied region holds some of the country's finest national parks, seashores, and wildlife refuges. Its treasures include the highest peaks and waterfalls in the East, the largest deciduous forest area in the East, and the longest cave system in the world.

The Upper South—encompassing the lands of Virginia, North Carolina, West Virginia, Kentucky, and Tennessee—is split down the middle by the Appalachian Mountains. In several major ranges running northeast to southwest, the central Appalachians hover over the region like a peaked roof. Water rolling off the east side finds its way to the Atlantic, while on the west side the rivers eventually drain into the Gulf of Mexico via the Mississippi. On both sides, a wide, forested peneplain—actually a low plateau in Kentucky and Tennessee—smooths gradually to sea level, or almost so in the west. The Appalachians were at one time as high or higher than the Alps, but over the course of millions of years they were worn down—chiseled and washed by wind and rain, cracked by ice and roots. Streams and rivers dug out steep canyons and wide valleys, steadily carrying away bits of the mountain like an endless demolition team. The Appalachians today have a creased and aged look; this is a face that has seen a lot of change.

With all of West Virginia and roughly one-third of Virginia, Kentucky, Tennessee, and North Carolina mountainous, much of the region's public land lies in the mountains, protected as national forest or national park. Nonetheless, while windswept mountaintops have their share of appeal, some of the greatest beauty spots in the country are found along the Virginia-Carolina coast and elsewhere in the Upper South.

In fact, many of the region's most memorable wildlands are no farther than a backyard. There was a tract of woods behind our house in Raleigh, North Carolina, where I grew up. One spring when I was a boy I went back there and collected 50 different kinds of wildflowers. With a field guide and my mother's help, I identified the wood lily, lady's slipper, larkspur, mountain laurel, morning glory, jewelweed, maple-leaved viburnum…. Their names only added to the mystery and beauty that I'd hardly noticed until a school science project made me pay closer attention.

I'd noticed the woods, though. There were a lot of kids in the neighborhood, and the games and adventures we had back there were endless: hunting for crayfish, building dams, sledding, running from enemies—real and imagined. I knew the woods much better than I knew the world outside them. Even in dreams you'd head for the woods if you needed to escape— the woods were where it was safe.

There was a bigger woods a short drive from our house. William B. Umstead State Park held thousands of acres of Piedmont forest, and my parents took me and my brother and sisters there for picnics. We went on vacations to the warm North Carolina coast, where we saw porpoises leaping in the ocean and herring gulls cruising the surf line. With my father I went on overnight fishing trips down the Roanoke River and goose hunting to Currituck Sound and Lake Mattamuskeet. When I was a little older, I attended summer camp in the mountains near Asheville, North Carolina, where I backpacked up Mount Mitchell and took wild canoe trips down the Tuckasegee and Nantahala Rivers. Older still, I went on school trips to West Virginia—we climbed Seneca Rocks, hiked on North Fork Mountain, swam in cold mountain streams.

Not until I was grown did I really discover Tennessee and Kentucky, but they felt like old friends. The oak-hickory woods had a familiar look and feel—the worn mountaintops and misty ridges, the extravagant rhododendron blooms, the limestone caves and sandstone cliffs, the white-tailed deer and circling hawks. Only the Mississippi Delta area of those states was different from anything I'd seen.

I live now just east of the Blue Ridge in Virginia. I've seen rabbits, squirrels, chipmunks, groundhogs, deer, cardinals, bluebirds, jays, flickers, brown thrashers, grackles, crows, and robins—all from my window. Out in the yard I can see or hear hawks, turtles, wildflowers, 80-year-old oaks and beeches, pileated woodpeckers, wood thrushes, sparrows, great horned owls, chickadees, nuthatches, and more. And I don't even live in the country.

From the Mississippi to the Atlantic, city to country, the Upper South holds a tremendous variety of life. Sadly, many animals are visible because, crowded out of diminished woodlands, they have nowhere to go but into suburban neighborhoods. But it is in these remaining narrow tracts of woods that many children, including my own, will discover the natural world for the first time. If you love the land as a place of refuge and beauty, take some children to a forest park, to a seashore, or to the mountains. Many thanks to my parents, who did that for me.   –John M. Thompson

the Coastal Plain

"... wide, bird-frequented shores and mazy marshes ..."

Across the Coastal Plain of Virginia and North Carolina, rivers broaden as they meander through low fields and forests, slowly draining the land and emptying into the sea. In Virginia, the Potomac, Rappahannock, York, and James Rivers carve out three stubby peninsulas that jut into the Chesapeake Bay, the largest inlet on the Atlantic coast, while in North Carolina, the Roanoke, Tar, Neuse, and Cape Fear Rivers likewise ramble eastward from the rapids of the fall line—a geographic line where the rivers drop sharply from the Piedmont. An 80- to 130-mile-wide sweep of flat land, the Coastal Plain encompasses pristine barrier islands, primitive swamps, and lush coastal forests. Roads trail out to the ends of peninsulas, where nature takes over in thickets and marshes, estuaries and bays.

Preceding pages: Sunset melts across the marshes of Chincoteague National Wildlife Refuge in eastern Virginia. Opposite: A wild foal takes a breather in the spongy grasses of the refuge's South Wash Flats.

With the exception of the areas surrounding Virginia Beach, Virginia, and Wilmington, North Carolina, the region remains largely rural. The inlets and coasts of these two states were among the first places settled in the New World; however, fierce storms, shallow waters, and tough growing conditions pushed the settlement wave farther west, leaving much of the Coastal Plain with a lingering look of newness. It is tough to pick favorites, but after countless visits I'd have to say this is one of my favorite ecoregions of the Upper South. These wide, bird-frequented shores and mazy marshes got into my veins at an early age, and I expect them to stay there a lifetime.

A 37-mile-long barrier isle named Assateague Island fronts the Atlantic on the Delmarva Peninsula at the north end of the Upper South's Coastal Plain. Native Americans appreciated the plentiful fish, oysters, clams, crabs, and waterfowl of Assateague, but they generally came for short visits only. The insects, wind, heat, and lack of drinking water made this narrow island poorly suited for human occupation. European settlers equally found the isle uninhabitable. For the most part, as far back as the 17th century, they only ventured ashore to enjoy the bounty of the area's waters and try some farming. In addition, they grazed their livestock on the island to avoid the fencing and taxes required on the mainland; the island's wild ponies are descended from those early herds. Pirates the like of Blackbeard sheltered in the island's protective coves, and hunters and egg collectors profited from Assateague's astounding multitude of shorebirds, wading birds, and migratory waterfowl.

By the early 1900s a few hardy individuals had established homes, a school, and a store; a fish-processing factory operated at Toms Cove in the 1920s. But these had all disappeared by the 1940s, when developers were taking a good long look at Assateague, hoping to build seaside communities. However, a severe storm in the late winter of 1962—one that stranded boats in the streets and yards of the town of Chincoteague on neighboring Chincoteague Island—convinced people that Assateague was best left wild, paving the way for the creation of Assateague Island National Seashore in 1965.

The southern end of the island had already been set aside in 1943 as Chincoteague National Wildlife Refuge, to protect the sharply declining populations of snow geese and other birds. With the creation of the national seashore, the entire island was preserved and protected. Though some parts of the island are still open to off-road vehicles, you can today walk the length of Assateague and find no man-made structures other than minimal park and refuge facilities, a decommissioned Coast Guard station from 1922, and an 1867 lighthouse.

Chincoteague National Wildlife Refuge, a graceful collage of maritime forest, marshes, dunes, and beach, provides sanctuary for more than 320 species of birds and 30 species of mammals. Just the other side of the dunes, pelicans skim the crests of waves, flying aslant the wind. Known and loved for its wild ponies, this 14,000-acre

A great blue heron perches on the stern of a waterman's boat in a Delmarva Peninsula tidal creek. Fishing villages dot the peninsula's many waterways.

parcel, one of the most visited national wildlife refuges, not only extends over a good portion of Assateague—including a 12-mile sweep of wild beach open to foot access only—but also parts of other nearby barrier islands.

I recently took a walk on the Freshwater Marsh Trail, which meanders through prime wildlife habitat. From my vantage point atop an impoundment dike I took in wide views of the Snow Goose Pool, its water level lowered in summer to concentrate fish for wading birds and expose mudflats for shorebirds. The large pink and white blooms of rose mallow (a kind of hibiscus) decorated the trailside, and the round green leaves of pennywort carpeted the edges of the marsh. Ducks and geese fed on the seeds and roots of bulrushes, while red-winged blackbirds took flight from scrub trees, their bright scarlet epaulets flashing in a wonderfully big canvas of sky, marsh, water, and woods. A few sika elk browsed along the edges of the pool, and sometimes right along the roadside. The sika are an Asian species released here in the 1920s—they are smaller than white-tailed deer and have white spots year-round. I did not see any ponies, however. They live on another part of the refuge.

The famous ponies survive on beach grass, coarse salt-marsh cordgrass, and other salty vegetation that necessitates their drinking a lot of water. Two herds of about 150 animals each, separated by a fence, live on the Virginia and Maryland sides of Assateague island. To raise money, the Chincoteague Volunteer Fire Company in 1924 started a "Pony Penning" that has become a July tradition. Cowboys round up the ponies on the Virginia side of Assateague and herd them splashing into the

the Coastal Plain

Elegant hunters, great herons stalk breakfast in a reflecting pool at Chincoteague

National Wildlife Refuge, a favorite haunt of marsh and waterbirds in spring and summer.

channel; after a short swim, cheered on by thousands of spectators, the ponies emerge on the shore of Chincoteague, dripping wet. Most of the foals are auctioned off; the rest swim back to Assateague.

At the southern tip of Assateague, gulls, egrets, and migratory birds take to the salt marshes out at Toms Cove, a slender strand away from the ocean. Hooking south and west, portions of the five-mile strand are closed to humans from mid-March to September to protect threatened piping plovers and other beach-nesting birds. This is, after all, a refuge for wildlife.

In fact, much of the Virginia shoreline to the south is a protected chain of barrier islands belonging to the U.S. Fish and Wildlife Service and the Virginia Coast Reserve; the islands are either closed to the public or accessible only by private boat. Down here the Delmarva Peninsula narrows to a fingertip of land, pointing the way south for thousands of migrating waterfowl, shorebirds, songbirds, and raptors. In the warm months, herons and egrets take up residence in the high-grass marshes and tidal creeks, posing like leggy fashion models.

Down below the James River, in tidewater Virginia and North Carolina, the Great Dismal Swamp spreads along the inner coastal plain like a dark and mysterious kingdom. Though much of its ancient cypress forest was logged, the Great Dismal still harbors a good variety of plants and animals, including several rare species, within its thick vine-entangled woods.

It was Col. William Byrd II who dubbed it "dismal." He was surveying a line between the Virginia and North Carolina colonies in 1728, his party beset by chiggers, ticks, and flies. He declared that "never was Rum that cordial of Life, found more necessary than in this Dirty Place." When searching for epithets for the swamp he came up with "vast body of dirt and nastiness" and "horrible desart." George Washington, surveying in 1763, had a different outlook—he called it a "glorious paradise."

No matter what your experience and point of view, one thing is certain. The Great Dismal is no desert. It is a vast wetland forest, wrapped in vines and briars, home to bears, deer, bobcats, otters, frogs, turtles, and all manner of birds. The swamp once covered some 2,200 square miles, but logging and draining reduced it to about a quarter of that size. Ironically, Washington, who extolled the swamp's beauty, was one of the first people to exploit the Great Dismal. In the 1760s, his Dismal Swamp Land Company and Adventures for Draining the Great Dismal Swamp built the five-mile-long Washington Ditch. Dug by slaves, the ditch ran from the west side of the swamp to Lake Drummond. Soon realizing that draining the entire swamp was unrealistic, the various companies focused on hauling out cypress for shipbuilding and cedar for shingles. Washington wasn't pleased with the return he was getting, so he sold his share of the operation. But the logging continued.

In the Great Dismal Swamp, a hiker takes to the road along Washington Ditch.

A mammal common to tidewater Virginia and North Carolina, the intrepid raccoon can adapt to almost any environment, and can eat almost any food.

To transport the lumber and drain more land for farming, the 22-mile-long Dismal Swamp Canal was built in the 1790s; running north-south, it connects Virginia's Elizabeth River with the Albemarle Sound in North Carolina. The oldest continually operating canal in the country, the Dismal Swamp Canal is now on the National Register of Historic Places and forms part of the Atlantic Intracoastal Waterway. Before the Civil War, runaway slaves formed little self-sufficient colonies in the deep and gloomy reaches of the swamp, safely hidden from dogs and trackers. And still the logging went on, as well as road building. By 1976, more than 140 miles of roads had been constructed in the Great Dismal, and the whole swamp had been logged at least once. The roads, put in to help access the lumber, altered the natural flow of water across the land, and the ditches, dug for soil for roadbeds, helped drain the water. The result is a vastly changed swamp. The once dominant bald cypress, tupelo, and white cedar now make up only 20 percent of the forest; the red maple has taken over in the much drier conditions.

In 1973 one of the last private owners of the swamp, the Union Camp Corporation, donated 49,100 acres to the Nature Conservancy, which in turn donated the tract the next year to the U.S. Department of the Interior, for the establishment of a national wildlife refuge. The refuge, a noteworthy tract of hardwood and cypress swampland, protects nearly a third of the remaining Great Dismal Swamp. At its heart lies 3,100-acre Lake Drummond. Named for the first governor of North

Carolina, the oval lake averages only six feet in depth, its water stained to a tea color by the tannins in juniper, gum, and cypress bark. Though the lake's acidity keeps fish life at a minimum, the water has long been noted for its exceptional purity—stored in kegs on ships, it slaked the thirst of many a sailor in the 18th and 19th centuries. No one knows how the lake formed. Theories include a peat fire or a meteor that created a depression which later filled with rainwater. Even today, there are still reports of weird lights at night—fueling numerous sightings of ghosts and pirates throughout the years. In fact, the glowing lantern-like lights are probably the result of smoldering peat or ignited methane from decomposing vegetation.

Plants preserved in the refuge include the dwarf trillium, found mostly in the northwest part of the swamp; the silky camellia, also in the northwest as well as on hardwood ridges; and the rare log fern—an emerald green jewel—which is more prevalent here than anywhere else in the world. Among the refuge's more than 200 bird species are a variety of warblers, including the Swainson's, black-throated green, and prothonotary (swamp canary), which arrive en masse in spring. In winter huge flocks of blackbirds and robins swirl through the refuge forests. Bald eagles occasionally visit the refuge.

Walk in these woods and you'll feel as though you've stepped into a primeval landscape—where maples, gums, and mossy cypresses pinch out the light and deer tread lightly across the forest floor, almost invisible among the slender trunks in the shadowy understory. In summer the blooms of trumpet and passion vines add bright tones of orange and purple. Last spring I took a hike along the Washington Ditch Road, which runs arrow-straight alongside the water-filled channel. Otters glided through the ditch, great blue herons stood like sentries waiting for prey, and belted kingfishers darted and hovered above the surface.

Though there are fewer kinds of plants and animals in Great Dismal than there were originally, refuge managers are attempting to restore the swamp to something approaching its early diversity. Through water control, forest maintenance, and wildlife management and habitat restoration, the refuge hopes to return the swamp to an earlier version of itself, including more cypress and wetlands. But with continuing loss of surrounding areas to residential, commercial, and agricultural development, it faces an uphill battle.

Just a few miles southwest of the Great Dismal, a relatively new swamp is in the making. Shaded as the area is by moss-hung cypress and tupelo trees, it is hard to believe that North Carolina's 760-acre Merchants Millpond has not been here for ages. Not even 200 years old, the atmospheric millpond on Bennetts Creek was created in 1811 to furnish power for a sawmill and gristmills that operated in Gates County. Commercial activity around the pond came to an end just before World War II, and piece by piece the millers sold the land to developers. In the 1960s, an outdoor enthusiast from nearby Currituck County bought the pond and surrounding land from developers and later donated 919 acres to the state. His gift saved the pond and led to the

A red maple blazes before a scrim of mossy bald cypresses in Merchants Millpond.

establishment of Merchants Millpond State Park in 1973. The Nature Conservancy chipped in a comparable amount of land the same year.

Now the pride of Gates County, the park preserves the bayou-like millpond and the Lassiter Swamp section of Bennetts Creek, which feeds the pond. Spanish moss dangles from old bald cypresses, which stand knee-deep in the inky, acidic water. Resurrection ferns line the banks, while cow lilies and floating duckweeds stipple the surface of the pond, painting a scene of constantly changing colors, textures, and moods.

On drizzly days, raindrops ping the glassy surface of the pond, rippling the reflections of cypress knees and limbs. A heron flaps silently across the water, while crows and woodpeckers make heckling noises in the distant reaches of the forest. An otter peeks out of the murky water along the edge, then ducks away with scarcely a flutter on the surface. On other days, carpenter frogs, leopard frogs, and various tree frogs trill and croak, lending a voice to the primordial landscape; cooters and snapping turtles take the sun on partially submerged logs. Two ancient fish species, the long-nosed gar and the bowfin, coastal plain inhabitants for millions of years, cruise the pond waters. The alligator, another ancient species, has been spotted in the park only in the last few years. Rarely found this far north, the gators may have been released or they may possibly have migrated from a similar habitat to the south. If the latter, it indicates that Merchants Millpond has become a much-needed refuge for a variety of animals.

The Outer Banks are a long, penciled eyebrow of barrier islands sweeping out from the Albemarle and Pamlico Sounds. More than 125 miles of the banks are protected as national seashores. Bearing the relentless onslaughts of wind, currents, storms, and sun, the flora and fauna that live on the banks are hardy survivors. Shifting dunes up to 100 feet high shelter in their swales a surprising diversity of grasses and wildflowers—goldenrods tilt gently over bunches of tiny asters, while gaillardia and flowering pennywort create vivid little paisley-patterned gardens close to the ground. In a few places the islands are wide enough to support a sizable maritime forest, guarded on the seaside by high dunes and a weather-toughened front line of stunted cedars and live oaks. Southern species such as yaupon and dwarf palmetto grow under the protection of willows, gums, and pines. And songbirds, foxes, deer, and other creatures live on a slender margin, far from the mainland and only a few hundred yards from the high-tide line. During hurricanes and nor'easters the animals hunker down as best they can to ride out nature's fury.

Nags Head Woods Preserve is a 1,200-acre jewel of old-growth maritime forest—and one of the best-kept secrets of the Outer Banks. More than 300 kinds of plants grow in the species-rich forest, protected from the battering sea by an earthwork of ancient dunes. Huge hickories, oaks, beeches, and pines, some of them hundreds of years old, rule the old dune ridges, while black willow and gum trees preside in swampy swales. In addition, the water violet and the mosquito fern—both exquisite—thrive in these woods.

The Sweetgum Swamp Trail loops into various plant communities in the heart of the preserve. Yellow-bellied slider turtles edge toward a pond and disappear with small plops, pine warblers sing purposefully in the nearby woods, and rare wooly beach heather grows in the sandy areas about halfway around. The Roanoke Trail leads through a salt marsh, where waist-high cordgrass and black needlerush ripple in the breeze; the trail ends with an expansive view of Roanoke Sound. In summer, a small orchid called southern twayblade grows along the trail, as does the pink lady's slipper, also an orchid.

Windblown, barren, and mounded high, nearby Jockey's Ridge has the look and feel of a desert landscape. Its height of 80 to 100 feet gives the ridge ranking as the tallest sand dune system on the Atlantic coast. It sits at the southern end of a range of massive dunes that run all the way to Virginia. In dune-speak, Jockey's Ridge is a medano, a tremendous pile of shifting sand free of vegetation. The sand likely came from offshore shoals; hurricanes and other storms rob the shoals, depositing sand on area beaches where it later can blow inland.

Early seafarers used the high dune as a navigational landmark, but the origin of its name has been obscured over time. In all likelihood the appellation stems from the early 19th-century practice of racing wild horses along the base of the dunes. As Nags Head grew in the 20th century into a popular vacation destination, development began crowding Jockey's Ridge. In 1973 the area directly below the dune was targeted for residential development until a local woman actually put herself in front of a bulldozer. A preservation organization was formed on the spot. One year later the dune was designated a national natural landmark, and Jockey's Ridge State Park was established in 1975.

One of the interesting—and problematic—features of the dune is that it moves. Prevailing northeast winds in winter push the sand southwest. The opposite is true in summer, meaning the dune more or less should stay put. But over time, the general trend is toward the south. The dune wants to move. People want it to stay in place: A state park that moves three to six feet every year is going to start traveling over roads and buildings, creating havoc. In fact, with the hurricanes of the early 1980s, the dune pushed out 600 feet in some places and engulfed a putt-putt golf course. Roads and driveways are continually under threat from the 10.4-million-cubic-yard sand pile. The park service has already bought out six homes—one lot is now covered in sand. Other than chasing the dune, what's the solution? One obvious answer is to stabilize part of the dune with grasses, as was done on Kill Devil Hills in the late 1920s. Grass over the entire dune, though, would completely change the nature of the park, which is now a living, shifting mountain of sand. In the meantime, the park periodically hauls sand from the south

Cottages line the shore of Nags Head, as seen from the top of 100-foot-high Jockey's Ridge, the highest sand dune system on the Atlantic Coast.

side around to the north—most recently trucking 112,000 cubic yards at a cost of nearly $500,000.

But there's not much the park can do to restore the dune's diminishing height: Since 1974 the dune has lost about 20 feet. Though some people have speculated that surrounding development has blocked sand from replenishing the dune, or that erosion has been caused, at least in part, by tourists, most experts believe the relentless winds are simply redistributing the sand and thus flattening the dune. Regardless, the dune is expected to remain the dominant coastal feature for centuries to come.

The pull of the dune is irresistible—it is not a long walk to the summit, but the loose sand and the somewhat steep pitch of the east face offer a bit of a workout. Pretending I was on the final pitch of Everest, I slogged to the top, but really without much huffing and puffing. From there I had a wonderful panorama of the bare dune fields, the ocean, Roanoke Sound, and the cottages of Nags Head. The bright sails of hang gliders hung on the air—the steady, light winds and the gentle slope of the dune offer exceptional conditions for beginners. Not coincidentally, in 1903, Orville and Wilbur Wright made the first manned, motorized flights only a few miles north of here at Kill Devil Hills.

A 1.5-mile nature trail winds along the quiet northwest side of the dune's base. Unlike the dune itself, the low-lying areas have pockets of vegetation. Bushy clusters of bayberry, red cedar, and wax myrtle stand like little oases in a vast desert.

An Outer Banks sunrise colors the fringe of the Atlantic near Kill Devil Hills. The elements

inexorably shift and shape the 175-mile chain of North Carolina barrier islands.

brown pelicans

Just about any day on the Outer Banks you can see brown pelicans, usually in groups of a half dozen or more. Gliding with seven-foot wingspans, necks tucked in, they are reminiscent of the pterosaur, a winged dinosaur. They often work just beyond the breakers, diving like missiles from 30 feet and higher, crashing into the water and scooping up fish in their great pouches.

Once an endangered species throughout its range, the pelican has come back from the edge of extinction. In the 1950s and '60s, the population of brown pelicans and other birds plummeted. Researchers noticed that fewer chicks were being born because the eggs weren't hatching properly. Someone measured the thickness of the eggshells and compared them with eggs tucked away in museums, eggs from decades ago. It turned out the pelicans were producing eggs with thinner shells, so the chicks were hatching prematurely. Experiments showed that pesticides such as DDT were capable of harming eggshells. The Environmental Protection Agency banned DDT in 1972, pelicans stopped ingesting the toxic compound, and—it worked! Eggshells became thicker, and the number of pelicans in the Carolinas and elsewhere increased.

The brown pelican often perches on rocks or piles along the coast.

Lizards blend in with the greenery, and tracks of small nocturnal animals indicate an active nightlife in the park. Over by the sound, cattails and sedges prevail in the fresh-water marsh area, while salt-tolerant cordgrasses spread out along Roanoke Sound.

But for one family, the long lonely stretch of the Outer Banks protected by the Cape Hatteras National Seashore could have been different. Thanks to an artist named Frank Stick and his son David, it is here for all to enjoy in a nearly pristine state. Stick moved to Roanoke Island from New Jersey in the 1920s and proposed creating a national seashore. In the midst of the Depression, local leaders in eastern North Carolina thought Stick's idea would be great for the economy. Within a few years, bridges and paved roads had linked several islands, protective dunes were created with fences, and local historical attractions were being touted. But World War II stopped the project in its tracks. Then, motivated by what might lie beneath the surface of some sandbars, oil companies began offering landowners tempting deals before the national park service had mapped out a seashore plan. Stick had moved away, assuming his work here was done. With the national seashore now looking doubtful, his son, local historian David Stick, rolled up his sleeves and started garnering support. By 1952 he had gained the backing of two philanthropical organizations, and six years later a new national park was dedicated.

Now running for 70 miles like a bent arm with the elbow at Cape Hatteras, the seashore spans the middle of the Outer Banks, the part farthest from the mainland—some 30 miles of Pamlico Sound separate the mainland from the cape. The skinny chain measures only 200 feet wide in places, and about 3 miles wide at the cape. Motorists drive for miles and miles and see nothing but grassy dunes and flights of pelicans and gulls, with snapshots of the sound from time to time.

At the end of the last ice age, about 10,000 years ago, the sea level was 400 feet lower, and the coastline extended east much farther than it does today. As the ice melted, water washed over sand ridges created by wind and waves; the flooded area became the shallow Pamlico Sound, and the ridges, thus cut off from the mainland, became barrier islands. Scientists estimate that the islands once stood 40 miles farther out. They continue to migrate westward, though at only a few feet per year. During storms, water breaches the dunes, carrying sand from the front of the islands toward the back, hence the gradual move westward. Tropical hurricanes and mean nor'easters have also taken their share of boats and lives here. Yet longtime residents are generally unfazed by storms. They board up their homes and take a wait-and-see attitude, living in tune with nature's fury and frequently rebuilding what Mother Nature tears down. When Hurricane Isabel roared ashore in September 2003, it cut a new inlet from the Atlantic to the sound between Hatteras Village and Frisco, wiping out houses, motels, and the highway. A five-million-dollar project closed the one-third-mile gap within several weeks by pumping some 400,000 cubic yards of sand through six miles of underwater pipe.

Through storm and calm, the barrier islands buffer the mainland and make for a peaceful sound, a protective nutrient-rich nursery for many marine animals and migrating birds. Twice a day, tides pour through inlets, cleansing the tidal flats and flushing out the natural waste. Nearly 400 bird species have been seen at the national seashore. Spring and fall migrations bring tremendous numbers of shorebirds and songbirds, such as plovers, yellowlegs, and warblers. Shorebirds frequent ponds and tidal flats, while songbirds inhabit the wooded areas. Herons, egrets, terns, and skimmers abound in the summer, while ducks and geese mass here in the winter.

Summer also brings the return of the loggerhead sea turtles. The turtles have been nesting on these mid-Atlantic beaches for millions of years, but in the last century the majority of their breeding grounds have been lost to coastal development. Now a threatened species, the loggerhead can still breed in peace on the protected shores of Cape Hatteras. Because these beaches are undeveloped and off-limits to cars during the nesting season, the hatchlings do not have to contend with artificial lights, which can cause them to run the wrong way, or with tire tracks on the beach, which can trap them. Females lumber onto the beach two or more times from May to August, dig a hole up by the dunes, and lay about 100 eggs. In about eight weeks the hatchlings scramble out at night and make for the shore; those that are not picked off by gulls or crabs, or eaten by fish in their first year, can grow to several hundred pounds. In 20 to 25 years, the females will return to lay their own eggs. And the cycle continues.

The north end of Hatteras Island is occupied by Pea Island National Wildlife Refuge. Many years ago, experts say, most of the world's greater snow geese wintered in the Pamlico and Currituck Sounds. They craved the "dune peas" they found here, beans that came from little pink-flowering plants growing in the dunes. The Pea Island refuge was set aside in 1938 to help slow the population decline of the snow goose and other waterfowl. The geese here and in other places have made such a huge rebound that they are actually overcrowding their breeding habitat way up on the high Arctic tundra. But as a result of the comeback one can again see significant numbers of these birds. Each fall and winter the refuge hosts about 3,000 greater snow geese.

The refuge's North Pond Wildlife Trail traverses a half-mile dike between impoundments. Beyond a tunnel of stunted live oaks, it offers an easy promenade along North Pond, where American oystercatchers show off their flaming orange bills, black-necked stilts walk on spindly pink legs, and black skimmers scoop up fish as they glide over the water. Autumn brings in a number of raptors, including peregrine falcons, kestrels, merlins, and various hawks. In the cold months the pond is a convention center for ducks—gadwalls, black ducks, wigeons, pintails, green-winged teal, and other dabblers. Quite observers might also spot an otter or a raccoon as it makes its way through the tall grasses to the pond. The trail ends at an observation tower; the tower's platform is a great place for drinking in soothing views of the whole

Squeezing the tube: A surfer takes advantage of post-hurricane wind-driven swells common in September on Cape Hatteras National Seashore.

maritime mosaic—island-dotted ponds, sinuous salt marshes, the sound, and the distant line of the ocean. From here the dunes look like whitecaps.

This scene of tranquility contrasts sharply with the scene of destruction found farther south. In the days of big sailing ships, the shoals of the mid-Atlantic states were considered the graveyard of the Atlantic. Risking everything for the good north and south currents along the shore, hundreds of ships have been stranded and wrecked off the coast. The treacherous and ever shifting Diamond Shoals off Cape Hatteras alone claimed dozens of ships—from dories to schooners, and brigantines to steamers. Lighthouses such as the renowned Cape Hatteras—a 208-foot-tall beacon with distinctive black and white spiral stripes—now help minimize the danger to shipping. In 1999 the lighthouse was moved inland 2,900 feet, about the distance it stood from the high-tide line when erected in 1870. Beach erosion over the years had left it only 200 feet from the surf.

From the lighthouse, the Buxton Woods Trail traipses through the state's largest maritime forest. In places the barrier islands are too narrow to support anything more than a beach, dunes, and marsh. Here at the cape, though, the island widens to three miles and rises to 50 feet, wide enough to establish a buffer of plants that can withstand the relentless wind and salt spray of the ocean and high enough to drain flood

the Coastal Plain

A tidal creek channels its way through a salt marsh to Core Sound on Cape Lookout National

Seashore. The shallow waters of the sound serve as a nursery for a host of marine life.

The distinctively patterned Cape Lookout Lighthouse (opposite), towering over
the 1859 keeper's cottage, warns mariners off the hazardous shoals of the cape.
Nature's patterns are repeated in endless variations: Nearby dune swales harbor a
surprising variety of wildflowers, including the yellow-fringed gaillardia (above).

tides. Relict dunes are now green with small yaupon, cedar, and live oak. Some of the trees look half dead—in a natural adaptation to the harsh winds, the seaward branches are bare bones. Dwarf palmettos grow here at their northern range, and tiny deer forage in these woods—on an island 30 miles from the mainland.

On Ocracoke Island—the next island south in the chain—the short Hammock Hills Nature Trail explores a younger forest than the Buxton Woods. Moving from scrub thicket into pine forest, the trail opens here and there to sandy patches that support prickly pear cactus. A viewing platform just off the sound takes in a wide marsh anchored by black needlerush and salt marsh cordgrass; the decaying plants feed a chain of life that includes oysters, clams, crabs, and fish. At sunset the low light from the sound bronzes the water and the grasses, erasing the distinction between the elements—sky, water, and land meld into one.

Even more dramatic and remote, the Cape Lookout National Seashore, only 15 minutes from the mainland by boat, lies far enough beyond the modern world to hearken to its own natural rhythms. The tides, the seasons, and the migrations of birds are the constants, upon which weather plays infinite variations. Over time, the islands shift, inlets close and open, but the changes here are made almost exclusively by nature instead of man. The main concession to convenience is the presence of some motor vehicles, mostly used by fishermen, on the beach or the sand road behind the dunes. Ongoing debate may someday come down in favor of a completely natural seashore, but in the meantime it is still possible to walk for miles or sit for hours and see few, if any, passing vehicles.

An international biosphere reserve, the 56 miles of seashore encompass the attenuated barrier islands called north and south Core Banks, as well as Shackleford Banks, a barrier island at right angles to the fishhook of Cape Lookout. Behind these main islands lies a complicated network of marshes and tiny sound-side islands. About 125 feral horses live on nine-mile-long Shackleford Banks, descendants of livestock owned by people who lived on the island until the 1890s. Averaging only 10 to 13 hands high (from ground to withers, one hand being 4 inches), the "horses" are technically ponies, but locals have long referred to them as horses or mustangs.

The village of Portsmouth was established on the north end of Core Banks in 1753. Situated at the mouth of Ocracoke Inlet, the village became a busy lightering port—that is, a center for lightweight, shallow-draft barges that loaded and unloaded ships too large to navigate through the inlet to the sound. After the Civil War, a change in shipping routes brought the gradual decline of Portsmouth. Since the early 1970s it has been predominantly a seasonal town; it became a 250-acre historic district when the national seashore was established in 1976.

I took a boat across from Harkers Island to Core Banks and was pleased to discover that there are no trails in the park. Instead, a boardwalk crosses the dunes, and then miles of empty beach stretch in either direction. North about 18 miles lies New Drum Inlet, separating north and south Core Banks. Three miles south is Cape Point. Along here huge flocks of sandpipers hunt tiny shellfish by the surf, twisting their heads nervously at interlopers on their private beach; waves send them sprinting away so fast their feet hardly touch the ground. Gulls and pelicans appear as winged shadows on the sand before swooping overhead. Here and there wire cages sit atop sea turtle nests to protect them from predation by raccoons; baby turtles are small enough to get out in their nighttime dash to the sea. In the cooler fall weather, some turtles hatch out in the morning, making them easier targets for gulls. One morning on a mid-October walk here, I found a hatchling struggling to reach the ocean. Amazed that a gull had not grabbed it, I picked it up and walked it over to the surf. Within a few seconds, it was gone.

Just inland from the lower Banks, places like the Croatan National Forest and Lake Waccamaw State Park hold dwindling stands of bald cypresses, strung with Spanish moss and standing knee-deep in water. Lake Waccamaw, a Carolina bay, contains numerous endemic freshwater species and harbors the rare and fascinating Venus flytrap. No one knows exactly how the mysterious basins called Carolina bays formed. Hundreds of these northeast-southwest-aligned oval depressions, ranging from less than an acre to more than 1,000 acres, pock the Coastal Plain of the Carolinas. Meteor showers, underground springs, and ocean currents and wind-and-wave action are among the more likely suspects, but so far no single theory has won the scientific community over. What is known is that Lake Waccamaw is the largest water-filled Carolina bay at a whopping 9,000 acres. The "bay" part of Carolina bay refers not to the water, but to the presence of sweet bay, red bay, and loblolly bay trees in and around the depressions. Most Carolina bays, in fact, are filled with vegetation; this one happens to be filled with water.

Another unusual aspect is that, while most Carolina bays are too acidic to contain much aquatic life, Lake Waccamaw has limestone bluffs along its north shore that neutralize the water enough to support a variety of plants and animals. The shallow, amber waters of the lake hold 11 species of snails, 15 species of mussels, and more than 50 species of fish, including at least 3 endemics—the Waccamaw killfish, Waccamaw darter, and Waccamaw silverside, each of them about two to three inches long. Numerous migratory waterfowl parachute onto the lake in winter, and in summer such birds as white-eyed vireos and northern parulas fill the woods with song.

Just to the east, palmettos grow near the shore around Wilmington, signaling a transition to the coastal plain of the Deep South. Here between the Carolinas, there is a hint of the subtropics in the softness of the air and the lushness of the vegetation. If there is a more lovely place on Earth than the Carolina coastal plain, I'm not aware of it. ❧

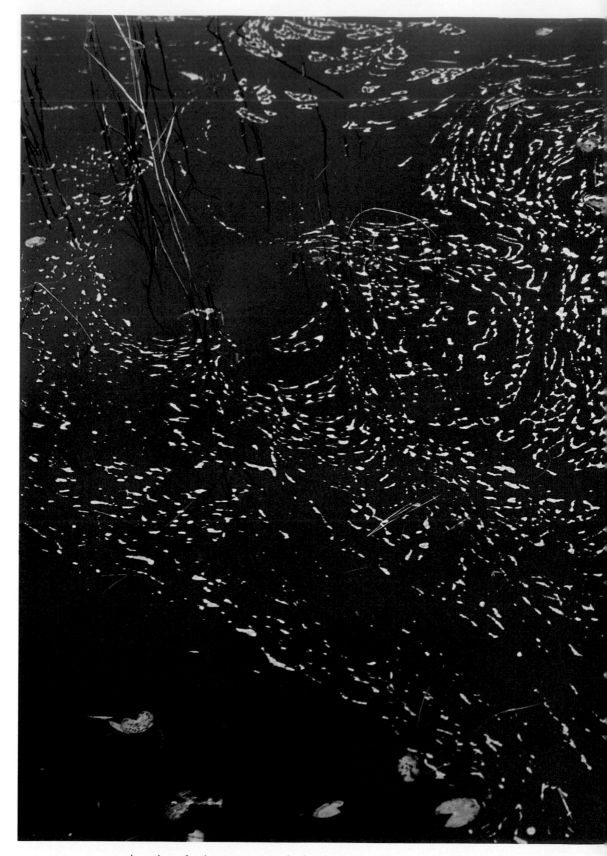

At the edge of Lake Waccamaw, the largest water-filled Carolina bay, wind-driven foam

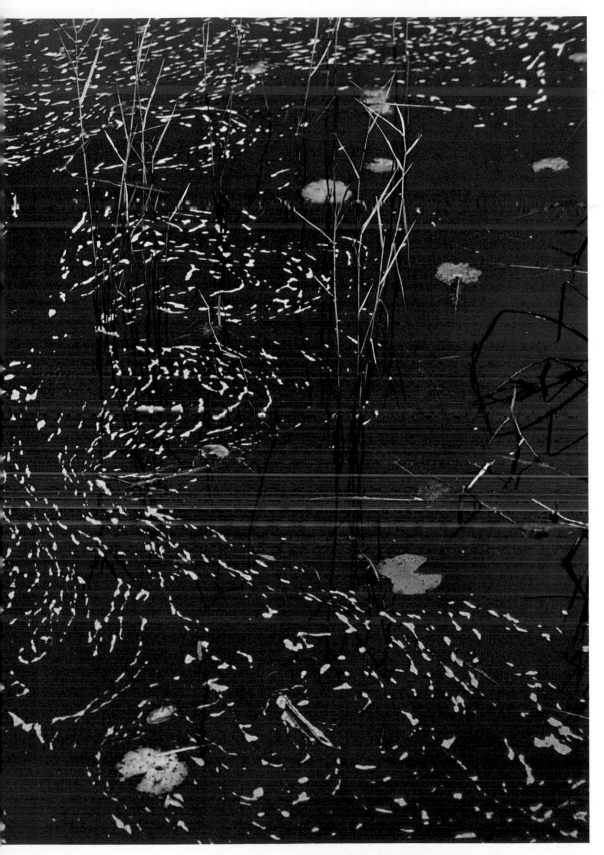

swirls among water lilies . These depressions are named for associated bay trees.

small gems
of the Coastal Plain

Back Bay National Wildlife Refuge in southeastern Virginia is a thin strip of land buffering Back Bay from the Atlantic Ocean. In the refuge's ample marshlands, the area's chain of marine life begins with shrimp, crabs, and small fish. Back in the shrubs and woods, white-tailed deer, marsh rabbits, and red and gray foxes find refuge, while raptors patrol above the loblolly pines and live oaks. Shorebirds and ghost crabs make a living out on the windy beach.

Fall and winter are the busiest bird seasons, when thousands of geese, tundra swans, and ducks set their wings over the inviting waters and marshes of Back Bay. The sight of a large flock of geese taking to the air in the early morning, wings beating furiously and reedy voices urgent, is a heart-pounding thrill. The marshes are particularly attractive at the end of the day, with sunlight melting over the water and wading birds riveted to their long shadows amongst the widgeon grass and wild celery.

A rare green sea turtle rests near Virginia Beach.

A cold wind whips off the open Chesapeake Bay on a November day in Kiptopeke State Park.

Kiptopeke State Park in eastern Virginia boasts the "Kiptopeke Navy"—a breakwater formed by nine World War II ships that were grounded here 1,500 feet from shore and filled with sand and water. Over the decades the breakwater has altered wave and current action so much that a good-sized beach has formed. The waters of the bay are just right for cooling off on a hot summer's day. The 1,000-foot-long fishing pier pushes out closer to the ships, which have formed reefs for numerous species of fish. Several boardwalks cross from an upland hardwood forest to scenic views of the Chesapeake Bay. In the fall the park operates a bird banding station to collect data on migratory species. Hundreds of thousands of songbirds come down the funnel-like Delmarva Peninsula, and along with them their raptor adversaries. Mid-mornings from late September through early October are the best times to watch.

the Piedmont

"... thick forests of pine and oak blanket the region ..."

One of the best ways to get a feel for the Piedmont is to stand on Pilot Mountain in North Carolina. Hundreds of square miles of low, barely rolling hills spread out before you, the carpet of green ending abruptly at the mountains some 20 miles north but pushing on to a hazy horizon south and east. Sandwiched between the Blue Ridge and the Coastal Plain, the broad midsection of Virginia and North Carolina is the transition zone between the mountains and the shore. Thick forests of pine, oak, hickory, and tulip poplar blanket the region, hiding an understory of maples, dogwoods, laurels, and wildflowers. Long rivers like the James and the Great Pee Dee water the region, their tributaries and floodplains helping to support deer, foxes, raccoons, hawks, owls, songbirds, and much more.

Preceding pages: Wildflowers bloom in an urban meadow in Fairfax, Virginia. Opposite: On Theodore Roosevelt Island in the Potomac River, a maple snags the light of a late afternoon in fall.

From Pilot Mountain, the R. J. Reynolds building and other Winston-Salem landmarks are also visible, rising in the southeast, seemingly isolated in a vast forest. But it is only an illusion. For nearly three centuries the Piedmont has been the region of choice for Virginia and North Carolina's human population. The clay and limestone soil and the moderate climate combine to make the region the tobacco-production center of the nation. Farming and logging have reached practically every corner of the Piedmont, with many cutover areas now in various stages of forest regrowth. Still, even as the forest recovers, large tracts of the Piedmont are disappearing. A recent study estimates that some 14 acres of North Carolina's Piedmont vanish every hour—mostly from urban expansion.

Yet despite the growth of urban corridors, the Piedmont still holds huge forests and fields where wildlife can live unmolested, and more and more of these semiwild locales are being set aside as parks and preserves. From tiny Theodore Roosevelt Island to the generous spread of Prince William Forest, the protected areas are generally established for one of two reasons—to give people a break from urban living or to give the native plants and animals a break from people. Either way, both people and nature benefit. The landscapes tend toward the gentle and serene rather than the spectacular, but several places near the Blue Ridge do provide dramatic views of the topographical shift from mountains to foothills. Other areas capture the essence of the Piedmont forest—limited on long views, but filled with photo-worthy meadows, glens, rippling creeks, and tall trees. I've lived most of my life in the Upper South's Piedmont, and I can honestly report that this subtle region of woods and rivers is not to be overlooked.

Great blue herons, white-tailed deer, wildflower-dappled meadows, stream-laced hills, towering oaks, tulip poplars. To find such natural beauty in abundance anywhere is a treat, but in a big city it is a rare blessing. A long lozenge of green, Washington, D.C.'s Rock Creek Park ranks as one of the largest urban parks in the country. More than twice the size of New York's Central Park, this haven of wildlife and hilly woods has provided respite to capital city residents and visitors since 1890. Presidents Theodore Roosevelt and Ronald Reagan, the latter often enjoying the bridle trails, number among the park's devotees.

Native Americans lived in the area for more than 5,000 years, hunting and gathering fruits and nuts. They cleared fields with periodic fires in order to farm squash, corn, and tobacco, and they traveled from village to village by canoes made from tall tulip poplars. By the late 1700s, settlers had displaced the Indians and were steadily clearing out more woods and putting up creek-powered gristmills. In 1861, Union armies built 68 forts around Washington, D.C.'s perimeter to guard against Confederate attack; remnants of some of these forts lie within the park. After the Civil War, Rock Creek Valley was briefly considered as a salubrious site for a "summer"

wildflowers

Providing a visual banquet for hikers and other outdoor lovers, wildflowers in hundreds of varieties blanket the fields, forests, and streamsides of the Piedmont. One harbinger of spring, the bloodroot, a poppy, begins showing its orange-centered white flowers in rich woodlands as early as March. Possessing eight to ten petals, the 1.5-inch flower blooms briefly, opening only during daylight. Indians used the underground stem for a red dye. The cut-leaved toothwort, another small white jewel, grows in moist thickets; it has only four petals. At the other end of the scale, the diamond-in-the-rough jimsonweed grows up to five feet tall and is distinguished by its rank odor, its poisonous fruit and leaves, and its striking beauty. Sporting creamy, trumpet-shaped flowers, jimsonweed is often found in abandoned lots and barnyards.

Bellworts, members of the lily family, are common woodland flowers from April to June; their elongated yellow blooms hang like bells. In damp woods, thickets, and clearings, peel your eyes for tiny but dazzling spring beauties. With pink or lavender candy-stripe veins, these five-petalled blooms look similar to wood sorrel but are a bit smaller and have long instead of clover-like leaves. The pink lady's slipper, a wild orchid, grows in dry pine forests, its name taken from its bright pouch; the rarer yellow lady's slipper prefers a moister environment.

Arrestingly vivid, fire pinks bloom April to June in thickets and open woods.

Polished stones and wood line the banks of Rock Creek, which twists and turns for nine miles through Washington, D.C.

White House, but the location scout thought the area better suited for a public park. By the turn of the 20th century, the woods had begun growing back in, starting with such pioneer species as the Virginia pine, which later yielded to second- and third-growth species such as oak, hickory, beech, tulip poplar, and other big hardwoods.

Today, 85 to 90 percent of the park is woodland; it frames the winding course of Rock Creek just above its junction with the Potomac River. In addition to playgrounds and fields, there are nearly 20 meadows scattered about—openings where goldfinches feast on thistles and great horned owls pick off shrews and mice. In spring the woods bloom with dogwood, redbud, azalea, and wildflowers, and in autumn the burnt oranges and lemon yellows of fall spread throughout the park. Such beauty sometimes pays a price for city living—dogwoods infected with anthracnose and oaks hit by gypsy moths often cannot survive in areas where they are already stressed by pollution, competition with non-native species, and other urban pressures. Small accidents, such as a pesticide spill, can seriously unbalance an ecosystem as small as Rock Creek Park. Yet people, plants, and animals carry on as best they can, living in close proximity to each other.

Miles of trails crisscross the park, offering nature enthusiasts a wealth of opportunities to get away without ever leaving the city. On a recent visit I made a two-mile loop by crossing Military Road near the park's nature center, heading past the earthworks of Fort DeRussy, and walking up the cool corridor of Rock Creek to the old Milkhouse Ford. Instead of crossing the 60-foot-wide creek here, where it ripples over a concrete slab, I kept my boots dry by heading uphill, then taking a left at the Western Ridge Trail. For most of the way I had nothing but birdsong and the rustle of leaves to keep me company. Another time I strolled down the bike trail—which parallels the creek for several miles—to Rock Creek's juncture with the Potomac River, where Theodore Roosevelt Island looms on the horizon.

Sitting in the middle of the Potomac, Theodore Roosevelt Island is a delightful mix of upland forests, swamps, and marshlands. Screened from the city, numerous birds and small mammals make homes here, while the hum of traffic from Roosevelt Bridge and the thunder of planes overhead are the only obvious reminders of the island's urban setting. That and the lunchtime walkers and joggers, who love to frequent this half-mile-long oasis.

Roosevelt Island once hosted Native Americans, who used the island for fishing. In the early 1800s, Virginian John Mason built a brick mansion and planted extensive flower, fruit, and vegetable gardens; his family held the island until the 1830s, mainly using it as a summer retreat. Union troops were stationed here during the Civil War. The idea of turning the island into a memorial to Theodore Roosevelt started as far back as 1919 (the year of his death), finally coming to full fruition in 1967.

The island makes a fitting tribute to the conservation-minded President. Tucked away in the heart of the island like an ancient ruin stands a monumental bronze of Roosevelt flanked by limestone and brick terraces, fountains, and pools. Among the Roosevelt quotations inscribed on stone tablets is one that reads, "There is a delight in the hardy life of the open: There are no words that can tell the hidden spirit of the wilderness, that can reveal its mysterious melancholy and its charm. The nation behaves well if it treats the natural resources as assets which it must turn over to the next generation increased and not impaired in value. Conservation means development as much as it means protection." Whatever he meant by that last sentence and whether he would stick with it today, it is a fact that during his Presidency, Roosevelt established 18 national monuments, protecting such treasures as the Grand Canyon and Mount Olympus (now Olympic National Park).

Trails thread the island's woods and marshes. In the forest, yellow-shafted flickers and downy woodpeckers drill high branches for insects, while mockingbirds run through a litany of borrowed bird songs. A boardwalk enters the swamp and marshes on the island's east side—my favorite area—where herons hunt crayfish and butterflies flit among the cattails and high grasses. Offering a hint of southern climes, bald cypresses grow in the freshwater swamp, as do maples, ashes, hickories, and a number of huge, gnarled old oaks. And although the island is at a considerable distance from the bay, tides wash through the swamp and marsh—an interesting occurrence given the fall line is a mere 15 miles upriver.

And hardly a more dramatic example of the fall line exists than the Potomac's foaming, falling, cliff-studded Great Falls. The river—which rises in the Alleghenies in West Virginia and runs more than 300 miles to the Chesapeake Bay—constricts

A lone dogwood clings to the cliffs above Mather Gorge. Located on the Potomac upriver of

Washington, D.C., the roaring Great Falls are the capital area's most dramatic natural landmark.

The plumes of this magnificent great blue heron indicate it is a breeding adult.

here from a width of more than 1,000 feet to between 60 and 100 feet as it plunges 76 feet into Mather Gorge. The sight of the falls never fails to amaze me.

In the late 1700s and early 1800s, canals were built to allow riverboats to bypass the rapids and thus expand trade with the west. George Washington, ever the businessman, started the Patowmack Canal in 1785 on the Virginia side of the Potomac. Its five locks raised and lowered boats the height of the falls. Flatboats traveled the 190 miles between Cumberland and Georgetown in three to five days. After offloading the whiskey, tobacco, flour, corn, and iron, the boatmen would break up their boats, sell the timber, and walk home. The Patowmack Canal stopped operating in 1830 because of competition from the recently begun Chesapeake and Ohio (C&O) Canal on the Maryland side of the falls. The C&O was started in 1828 with the aim of connecting the Atlantic Ocean with the Mississippi River via Georgetown (in Washington) and Pittsburgh, Ohio. Twenty-two years later, the canal had only made it as far as Cumberland, Maryland, before construction was halted. The railroad eventually made the C&O obsolete, but the entire system remains as an artifact, protected as a national historical park. Remnants of the Patowmack and its locks—now mostly a dry shallow ditch—can still be seen as well.

Both sides of the river provide spectacular views of the frothy, roaring waters. There is much for the eye to focus on—a plunging curtain of river, dropping into a 25-foot-deep pool; eddies of green water whirling around craggy rocks, places where the undercurrent shoots faster than the surface, curling the water up into standing waves; tilted and fractured cliffs 100 feet high. Just below the falls, kayakers play in the eddies and climbers work their way up cracks in the rock walls of the gorge. One of my favorite pastimes at the falls is to hike the Billy Goat Trail on the Maryland side. It scrambles over high cliffs forested with oaks, cedars, papaws, and sumacs; in the springtime, jack-in-the-pulpits, Virginia bluebells, and trout lilies splash color over the forest floor, while songbirds fill the air with their trills.

It is an early morning in December on the Mason Neck Peninsula. A bald eagle takes to the air from its roost in a cliffside tree, skims the misty surface of the bay, seizes a fish, and then flies back to its roost. This scene was common here, less than 20 miles south of Washington, D.C., until the turn of the 20th century. Then logging, and later the use of DDT, began snuffing out the regional population of bald eagles. Sediments and other pollution began filling streams, nesting sites became hard to find, and residential development started coloring in the habitat map. But in the late 1960s, the Nature Conservancy and U.S. Fish and Wildlife Service started buying up land on this Potomac River peninsula. Today, a cooperative management area that includes two parks and a national wildlife refuge helps protect more than 6,000 acres of Mason Neck, providing valuable nesting habitat for the eagles, which rarely nest around humans. Nearly 50 eagles now winter in the area.

Sunset inflames a stand of pines along the Potomac River (above).
One of the first signs of spring in the Piedmont is the chorus of the spring
peeper (opposite). The male frogs creep from their hibernation logs,
climb swamp grasses or shrubs, and begin vocalizing—a high rising whistle
or trill that sounds like the tinkling of bells when the frogs sing in concert.

In early 1800s garb, a boatman in the James River Bateaux Festival relives the days when wooden craft carried cargo from up-country farms to Richmond and beyond.

In December the resident eagles begin their courting and spectacular aerial mating rituals—tumbling together with locked claws high in the sky. The monogamous parents both tend the nest, often returning to the same tree platform in succeeding years. The eaglets hatch in spring, and in early summer they test their wings and learn how to use their talons to catch fish. It can take an eagle up to five years to grow its full adult plumage. In late summer many adults leave, but other eagles—adults and juveniles that nested in other areas—often arrive in fall to try the winter here.

Bird-watchers who visit in the early mornings of colder months may glimpse one or more of these mighty raptors, which nest in the vicinity of Kane's Creek and Belmont Bay in Mason Neck State Park. The park's Kane's Creek Trail winds through a mature lowland forest of oaks, hickories, hollies, laurels, and tulip trees. Woodpeckers and songbirds animate the woods, while deer, red foxes, and turkeys make rare appearances. The highly scenic one-mile Bay View Trail snakes through marshes and along the bay's shore. The stroll across the marsh boardwalk is especially lovely. Ducklings hide from snapping turtles and hawks amid the cattails and wild rice; yellow spatterdock dapples the water, where beavers make their homes. Great blue herons and Canada geese wing their way over the open water of the adjoining bay.

If you travel a few miles down the Potomac River, you'll find yourself on the shores of Prince William Forest, the biggest tract of Piedmont forest in the national park system. Although the land is now thriving, it was not always the case. Tobacco farmers cleared and depleted much of the area's land over the course of three centuries, and at the turn of the 19th century the Cabin Branch Mine extracted pyrite from the land to manufacture gunpowder. During the Great Depression, the federal government purchased the then marginal land for public use and named it the Chopawamsic Recreation Demonstration Area; the Civilian Conservation Corps built roads, bridges, and rustic cabins to make a summer camp for urban children. When the U.S. went to war in 1941, the camp became a top-secret facility for training spies for the Office of Strategic Services, a precursor to today's CIA. The area returned to public use in 1948 and was renamed Prince William Forest Park.

Today loud bursts of artillery from neighboring Quantico U.S. Marine Corps Reservation may occasionally interrupt the peace, but more common are the cries of wood thrushes and the chatter of pileated woodpeckers. The park accommodates a wide variety of life forms. Scientists estimate that 7,400 acres is the minimum size for a forest to maintain stable populations of all the forest-breeding birds in the mid-Atlantic states. At 15,000 acres, Prince William has more than enough acreage. In the last 50 years, such species as hooded warblers and yellow-throated vireos have quit nesting in heavily urban areas like Rock Creek Park, but they remain common nesters here.

I once bicycled the 12 mile scenic drive that circles the interior of the forest, stopping for walks along the way. Instead of offering long views, the road tunnels through a thick forest—especially gorgeous in spring or fall—with sunlight flickering through a kaleidoscope of leaves that tumble in the wind. Quantico Creek and its South Fork tributary, fed by springs and streamlets, wind their way through the forest and spill over the fall line, barely etching the erosion-resistant igneous rock of the Piedmont and deeply carving the softer sedimentary layers of the Coastal Plain. Footpaths trickle from the road to little masterpieces, detailed with miniature cascades and beaver dams, mossy boulders and patches of wildflowers and bracken. Visitors in tune with the quiet of the forest can see deer dipping their heads for a drink from a cool stream, and afternoon sunlight filtering through a tall tulip poplar and finding, for a moment, a forgotten bank of ferns.

Once busy with wooden bateaux ferrying tobacco down to Richmond, the gentle James River is now a quiet haven for waterbirds, fishermen, and canoeists. The 350-mile James ranks as the longest river completely contained within one state. Situated on a bend about midway along the river's mountain-to-sea journey, James River State Park offers a glimpse of the area's character. The park encompasses three miles of riverfront, blufftop forests, rolling meadows, fishing ponds, and the lovely Helena's Island, which lies a few miles downriver. Monacan Indians once hunted and fished the area, and it still harbors a good variety of wildlife, including black bears, bobcats, deer, timber rattlers, black rat and copperhead snakes, smallmouth bass, catfish, gar, and migratory birds.

Fall leaves decorate the banks of a swift stream in Virginia's Prince William Forest. Freshwater

streams—often endangered ecosystems—shelter more species than do the world's oceans.

Tree-capped Pilot Mountain explodes from the low-lying Piedmont. The 20-story-high quartzite formation was an important geographic landmark for local Indians.

In my opinion the best view in the park is from Tye River Overlook: Verdant hayfields run to forested hills, while eagles and hawks police the skies over the mirror-smooth waterways of the Tye and James. The canal-straight Tye, which hits the James at an almost perpendicular angle, has cut out the high limestone bluff of the overlook. The alkaline soil of the limestone supports a stand of northern white cedar (arborvitae), which is extremely rare this far south.

Helena's Island may be a bit out of the way, but it is well worth the small inconvenience. Leafy willows, papaws, and paisley-barked sycamores overhang the high, sandy bank of the river. Mowed fields line the broad floodplain on either side. When we visited this peaceful little island, a friend and I had it all to ourselves. Some visitors choose to explore the island's edges by canoe, but we scrambled down the riverbank, picking our way carefully over the briars, and crossed to the upper end of the island at low water—about 100 feet across a rocky ford.

A victim of flooding, the teardrop-shaped island is characterized by a healthy growth of only a few species rather than by diversity. A mature black walnut forest presides over basswoods, box elders, and ashes; within the interior grow such wildflowers as wood sorrel, loosestrife, and evening primrose. Birdlife peaks on the island in spring and fall, with visits by ospreys, sandpipers, mallards, northern parulas, and green-backed herons. Cows were once herded across the river to graze on the island; there are no trails now, but we easily covered the 57-acre island in an hour or two.

Some mountains don't know when to quit. Even after several hundred million years of weathering, Pilot Mountain still looms 1,400 feet above the surrounding countryside. A massive tree-topped column of erosion-resistant quartzite, this towering monadnock stands like a survivor amid the rolling Piedmont plain.

Today a national natural landmark, Pilot Mountain once served as an orientation landmark for local Indians and settlers on their travels through the area. The Saura Indians called it Jomeokee for "pilot" or "great guide." As with so many of the region's natural areas, it was a group of concerned local citizens who organized the land purchases that saved the area from commercial development and led to the establishment of a state park. The park was dedicated in 1968, and two years later a 1,000-acre parcel along the nearby Yadkin River was added. A six-mile wooded corridor connects the two sections.

From the park's Little Pinnacle Overlook the Piedmont stretches in a wide flat arc east and south, with the buildings of Winston-Salem clustered 25 miles away, about halfway to the horizon. To the north and west the Blue Ridge Mountains rise up sharply from the Piedmont. All around lie some 3,000 square miles of North Carolina and Virginia. From the overlook, a short trail dips into a cool garden of rhododendron and laurel and ends at the base of a 200-foot-high riven fortress of stone called Big Pinnacle. The monolith features cavelike recesses, crinkled and fissured walls, and vertical slabs angling off from the main body like buttresses on a modern edifice. The guardian spirits of Pilot Mountain are the ever present, jet black ravens that kite above the treetops, low enough sometimes to make audible whooshes of air. Ravens usually are confined to the Appalachian Mountains in the southeastern states, but these cliffs close to the Blue Ridge make an ideal habitat. In fact, Pilot Mountain is one of the few confirmed raven nesting sites in North Carolina.

Despite its solitary appearance, Pilot Mountain belongs to the Sauratown Mountain range, visible to the east. The Sauratowns pop up in the middle of a flat plain, some 15 to 20 miles east of the Blue Ridge, like a sudden tidal wave. These "mountains away from the mountains," named for the Saura Indians, are muscled with steep cliffs, rocky promontories, and exposed knobs—quartzite-capped peaks on a long ridge that shoots up more than 1,500 feet from the surrounding plain. Hanging Rock State Park contains the highest of the Sauratown peaks. Here you'll find steeply falling streams cascading over ledges; white-tailed deer picking their way through an oak and pine woodland strewn with galax, fire pink, bird-foot violet, jewelweed, and the exquisite pink lady's slipper; and dramatic views extending to the horizon. The long low wall of the Blue Ridge, the vivid valleys of the Piedmont, and the rolling landscape of the park unfold in a spectacular panorama from high atop the observation tower of Moore's Knob. Pilot Mountain sticks up like a fountain of stone to the west, and down below lie rafters of craggy cliffs. With the wind piling in from the west, you almost have the illusion of sailing on a mighty ship. ❧

Rising 17 miles southeast of the Appalachians, the jutting cliffs of Hanging Rock

provide superlative views of Moore's Knob and the flat Piedmont in the distance.

A long-exposure shot gives Window Falls on Indian Creek in Hanging Rock State Park, North Carolina, a supernatural glow (opposite). Farther downriver, a rhododendron blossom (above) lies caught in a tree stump. The creek flows through one enchanting scene after another as it traverses the park, which preserves part of a unique ridge that rises 1,500 feet from the Piedmont plain.

small gems of the Piedmont

Eno River State Park helps preserve one of the headwaters of the Neuse River. The Eno corkscrews through 33 miles of the Piedmont on its way to the Falls Lake reservoir; passing just north of Durham, it provides a corridor of tranquility for people from the city. After the Eno, Shakori, and Occoneechee Indians vacated the area, white settlers established mills and farms up and down the length of the river. When the city proposed damming it to create a reservoir in the mid-1960s, locals rallied to save the historic river and formed the Association for the Preservation of the Eno River Valley. The Nature Conservancy joined the fight and helped buy land in 1975 for the creation of a state park. Thanks to those efforts, visitors now stroll through a haven of pine forest and meadows accompanied by the sibilant murmur of the stream.

Cliffs 400 million years old dwarf hikers in Raven Rock State Park.

Raven Rock State Park takes its name from the throngs of ravens that once nested on the rock cliffs towering over the Cape Fear River here along the North Carolina fall line. More than a mile long and 150 feet high, the mica schist cliffs form the centerpiece of this park, which preserves a valuable piece of the vanishing Piedmont forest. Ravens may not roost in such large numbers as they once did, but wood ducks, owls, and woodpeckers still find shelter in the trees, while hawks scan the forests for mice, rabbits, salamanders, and other prey. Weasels, muskrats, beavers, and deer are among the mammals that live in the woods and along the streams, which teem with bluegill, green sunfish, snapping turtles, and yellow-bellied sliders.

Roots grope like tentacles over the rocky soil of Eno River State Park.

the Shenandoah

"... the promise of cool air, stream-lashed ravines, ..."

I often drive I-64 westbound from Richmond through mile after mile of central Virginia's verdant but flat terrain. Then, just before Charlottesville, I crest a hill and there in the distance rises the long low wall I am looking for: the Blue Ridge, the easternmost rampart of the ancient Appalachians. This line of highlands beckons with the promise of cool air, stream-lashed ravines, free-roaming wildlife, and grand views. In 1901, U.S. Secretary of Agriculture James Wilson was so moved by the beauty and commercial potential of the southern Appalachians that he proclaimed: "These are the heaviest and most beautiful hardwood forests of the continent. In them, species from East and West, from North and South, mingle in a growth of unparalleled richness and variety.... The preservation of these forests is imperative."

Preceding pages: A woodland face emerges like a familiar spirit from a tangle of briars in Shenandoah National Park. Opposite: The world begins in sunrise, vanquishing mist from Otter Lake, off the Blue Ridge Parkway.

By that time, much of the region's forest was falling fast to the ax. By all accounts, the woods and wildlife were well thinned out when many of the region's parks and forests were set aside in the 1930s. But second- and third-growth trees began filling in and deer, bear, and other animals began trickling back from hiding places in surrounding areas. Today, though of sparse human population compared with the Piedmont, Virginia's highlands have more roads and people than ever before. Yet the wild things persist: the deer browsing a mountain meadow, the great horned owl hooting in the dark, the yellow lady's slipper tinged by a setting sun in a forgotten grove high and hard to find....

Preserving an extraordinarily scenic section of the Blue Ridge Mountains, popular Shenandoah National Park straddles the ridge at one of the narrowest points in its Pennsylvania-to-Georgia run. The Piedmont rolls east from this razor-thin eastern flank of the Appalachians; the verdant Shenandoah Valley, for which the park was named, lies to its west. Beyond the valley, the 40-mile train of Massanutten Mountain parallels the Blue Ridge, and in the far distance rise the hazy mounds of the Alleghenies in West Virginia. Not to be confused with any feature in the park, Shenandoah Mountain is part of the Alleghenies, west of the valley.

The Blue Ridge has eroded over the past 250 million years from near-Himalayan stature to a low, serene series of parabolas and spur ridges that gently ramp down to forested valleys. The oldest, or basement, rocks in the park date back about a billion years. Uplift occurred over the course of several millennia and severely rearranged the order of some layers: Today some of that basement granitic rock is exposed on Old Rag Mountain. Greenstone, another interesting geologic feature, formed after repeated lava flows amassed layers some 2,000 feet thick. Crescent Rock and Little Devil Stairs show evidence of the polygonal columnal jointing that happened after the lava cooled and hardened.

Thick forests of red oak, white oak, hickory, maple, and pine swathe the entire park, with the exception of some highland meadows. Some of the lands were cut for farms and pastures in the 19th century, but since the dedication of the park in 1936, a thriving forest has filled back in. During photosynthesis, the trees release a vast number of hydrocarbon molecules, which refract enough sunlight to create the blue haze that perpetually hangs over the mountains, giving the ridge its name. Also, as in the Smokies to the south, dense fog and mist can gather in the valleys when warm air rides above a layer of cold air, creating little island peaks; the veil slowly lifts with the morning sun. Fall splashes the hillsides with such brilliant hues that the park's Skyline Drive has become a requisite tour for foliage lovers. In winter, the bare branches can become glazed with heavy ice, and snowfalls often close down sections of the road. Spring and summer bring life back to the park with the blooms of azalea and dogwood, mountain laurel and wild orchid.

Captivated by the timeless rolling mountains, a visitor drinks in the sunset from Skyline Drive, the popular parkway that winds 105 miles atop the Blue Ridge.

With the spread of settlement in the 1800s came the demise of many animals in the Blue Ridge Mountains. Larger animals such as bison, cougar, elk, and wolf were the first to go. By the early 1930s, deer, black bear, and wild turkey were almost nonexistent east of the Shenandoah Valley. Stocking of white-tailed deer in protected areas has led to an incredible comeback. Today it is hard to imagine the woods were not always filled with deer—you can scarcely visit the park without seeing at least one. The bears began coming back on their own in the late '30s, either down from Pennsylvania or across the mountains from the west. They now number several hundred. Some 200 species of birds have been recorded in the park, including numerous thrushes, warblers, and flycatchers. The annual mid-September migration of hawks is a spectacular event—you can often count 3,000 to 4,000 hawks in a single day from some exposed peaks and ridges.

Situated close to the Washington, D.C., metropolitan area, Shenandoah National Park is a favorite retreat for the urban weary, and it faces the continual challenge of offering a satisfying outdoor experience to an increasing number of visitors. Pollution from a variety of industries to the west has contributed to a substantial decrease in visibility—down from an estimated high of 115 miles to less than 25. The associated acid rains stress many trees already hit by blights. A recent report by the Boston-based Clean Air Task Force underscores the economic advantages of cleaner air, in the hope that an appeal to local purses is the most direct route to a healthier park.

the Shenandoah

Just west of Ramsey's Draft, morning mist rises from a valley near Bull Pasture Mountain. Fall

burnishes the area's forests in striking tones of burnt orange, blood red, and lemon yellow.

Lichen-covered boles (above) punctuate fall foliage in Shenandoah National Park. After an October frost, ferns in the George Washington National Forest (opposite) begin to wither and die. In the spring, tender coiled fronds called fiddleheads emerge from the fern stem; some fiddleheads are considered delicacies.

But on a clear spring or fall day at one of the overlooks, it is easy to forget the park's problems and just stare in awe at the miles of rippling blue-green scenery. Living a half hour east of the park, I know the pull these mountains can have. Shenandoah is wild enough for nearly 40 percent of it to be a designated wilderness. In balance, then, the national park has come a long way since its establishment nearly 70 years ago.

Skyline Drive runs for 105 miles down the length of the park. Peppered with scores of overlooks, the drive offers stunning views east and west, and access to the park's 500-mile trail system and other points of interest. The section between mileposts 39 and 46 includes some of the best hikes in the park. Just beyond milepost 39, the parking lot for Little Stony Man is the start of a great short walk up the rocky east side of the ridge and then over to Little Stony Man Cliffs, which have a dramatic western exposure. Less than a mile farther up stands the top of Stony Man Mountain, the park's second highest peak at 4,011 feet. From here there's an exquisite panorama of the valley and the long line of the Alleghenies to the west. The creased and folded mountains of the Blue Ridge span into the horizon north and south. Raptors ride the updrafts over a talus slope of huge rocks, while to the rear a forest of stunted cedar, northern red oak, striped maple, yellow birch, and laurel mixes with cold-living red spruce, balsam fir, and white pine at this high-elevation transition between southern and northern ecosystems.

Just south on Skyline Drive hikers can take a trail into Whiteoak Canyon, a place filled with gorgeous waterfalls and perilously high cataracts. Another nearby Blue Ridge classic—one I've done many times—is the hike up Old Rag, a tough but wonderful seven- or eight-mile circuit, best approached from the east side of the park. Near the top, the trail scrambles over and squeezes through a jumbled heap of huge granite boulders, offering thrilling views in all directions.

Yet another essential Shenandoah walk zigzags to the top of 4,050-foot-high Hawksbill Mountain, the highest peak in the park. The trail makes a moderately steep one-mile ascent through a forest of oak and ash, where owls hoot in late afternoon and deer nibble on leafy plants. A stone observation platform on the summit affords a near-360-degree panorama of blue mountains, craggy cliffs, and wide valleys—a mesmerizing picture of ancient geology domed by an infinite sky. Late afternoon shadows etch the hills and declivities in sharp relief.

Located in the middle of the park, the Big Meadows area is a tremendous spread of grasses and flowering plants covering several hundred acres. Indians camped and hunted on this high plateau, perhaps keeping it clear with regular fires. Since the establishment of the park, forest has reclaimed much of the meadow, but the park service does its best to keep the heavy growth in check with mowing and controlled burning. The south end of the park contains a number of fine walks and vistas. I like to hike up Turk Mountain just before sundown. Two miles up, the hike ends on a rocky summit with superlative views of the Blue Ridge spine, the valley, the

American beech

One of the region's most handsome shade trees, the American beech (*Fagus grandifolia*) makes an aesthetically pleasing sight whether on a city sidewalk or quiet mountain slope. The smooth light-gray trunk, often the target of initial carvers, rises to a soaring domed crown of leafy branches. The serrated, pointy leaves are light green underneath and measure about two to six inches—in fall look for them to turn a uniform brilliant yellow. They brown in winter, often hanging on well into spring. A long-lived tree, the American beech grows up to 80 feet in height, about average for the beech family, which includes oaks, chestnuts, and chinquapins.

Wildlife and people appreciate the fall crop of beechnuts, little triangular nuts that grow in pairs in prickly burs or husks. Every few years, a tree will produce a bumper crop, dropping plenty of food for squirrels, chipmunks, bears, birds. On your next autumnal foray, choose a nut that has grown enough to split its brown casing, peel away the casing with your thumb, and enjoy the sweet taste.

Decked in autumn glory, American beeches color the forests of the Shenandoah.

Morning fog paints a primordial scene on the upper James River near the Blue Ridge

Parkway. Some of the fog may have a modern source—a pulp mill downriver.

Alleghenies, and the Piedmont. And as often as I can I take my children up Little Calf Mountain, an easy hike with a big panorama and a picnicking meadow for a reward. You couldn't ask for better places to watch a sunset and to feel the enduring power of these old mountains.

One of the largest holdings of public land in the East, the combined George Washington and Jefferson National Forests sprawl throughout the mountains of Virginia, spilling across the borders of West Virginia and Kentucky. In the north, the George Washington forest covers large portions of the Allegheny, Shenandoah, Massanutten, and Blue Ridge ranges; to the south, the Jefferson forest includes Virginia's highest peak, Mount Rogers. Within these vast holdings are more than 40 tree species—about 80 percent of them hardwoods—and some 2,000 species of shrubs and herbaceous plants.

Scotch-Irish and German settlers began pouring into the Shenandoah Valley in the early 18th century, clearing its forests for farms and pushing up into the hills. In the next century, more and more forestland gave way to timber companies and iron furnaces. Slopes started eroding, streams clogging up with silt. With the forest went wildlife—elk, deer, and wild turkey were practically eradicated from the area. Lands in northern Virginia were among the first purchased as part of a federal forest reserve system in the early 1900s. In 1917, three units were collectively designated as the Shenandoah National Forest; in 1932 it was renamed the George Washington National Forest.

In southwestern Virginia, similar events were occurring: As soon as Congress allowed it, the government bought vast tracts of woodlands to set aside as forest reserves. But the woods were cut for timber as quickly as they were acquired. From the early 1900s to the mid-1930s, more than 63 percent of the current Jefferson National Forest fell to the logger's saw. The Jefferson forest was created in 1936; shortly afterward, the chestnut blight obliterated the region's dominant tree, destroying huge tracts of the remaining forest. But over time, with more careful stewardship, the forests and their wildlife returned. Of course, timber production is still a big part of the multiple-use policy. Nearly 34 percent of the George Washington and Jefferson is potentially available for logging; however, most of the tree cutting is done to provide wildlife habitat or to improve the health of the forest. Some 6 percent, or about 160 square miles, is completely protected as wilderness.

Split in two by Shenandoah Valley, the forest's Lee District lies the closest to Washington, D.C.—consequently, it receives a relatively high number of visitors. Forty-mile-long Massanutten Mountain dominates the east side of the valley; Great North Mountain looms tall on the west side. My favorite hike on the west side climbs six miles along the Virginia–West Virginia border to the top of Big Schloss (German for "castle"), a huge rock outcrop. The views are simply magnificent from

The serene shores of Abbott Lake at the Peaks of Otter Lodge entice travelers on the Blue Ridge Parkway to stop and reflect on the surrounding beauty.

the summit: Wooded mountains drop off both sides of a thin ridge and peaks rise in the far distance. I've done the 12-mile loop as an overnight, but the last time I was there my friends and I made a wonderful day hike out of it, and afterward we relaxed our sore muscles in the quaint town of Woodstock.

Picking up where Skyline Drive ends, the Blue Ridge Parkway runs for some 217 miles through Virginia on its way to North Carolina, passing through some of the state's most brilliant scenery. The George Washington forest flanks the parkway from about Waynesboro to Roanoke, allowing motorists to do more than just stretch their legs at an overlook.

A few miles south of Waynesboro, Humpback Rocks offers a quick, if somewhat steep, way to sample the ageless beauty of the Blue Ridge. The trail climbs smartly from 2,360 feet to 3,210 at the rocks, west-facing cliffs that provide grandstand views of the Shenandoah Valley and the distant Alleghenies. The cliffs are composed of greenstone, a grayish-green rock metamorphosed from ancient lava flows. Great in any season, the hike is especially pleasant in spring when thousands of rhododendrons and azaleas cheer up the understory; fall, of course, is justifiably the most popular time for Blue Ridge touring. The mountainsides seem to burn with the vivid yellows, oranges, and reds of a forest preparing to shed its coat of leaves.

On my most recent visit, my children were just old enough to come along—they had no trouble with the climb, but I still kept a close eye on them as they scrambled over these steep, well-worn cliffs.

I never tire of the long views found atop the Blue Ridge in this area; however, I relish the equally spectacular scenery of Crabtree Falls, a series of five exuberant cascades that together rank as one of Virginia's highest falls. A trail follows Crabtree Creek, pausing at four overlooks. One morning I took a walk here with a friend who is an environmental consultant; he helped me identify a number of plant species. From the parking lot, it was an easy stroll to the first waterfall, but peering 1,500 feet up the narrow ravine only made us want to climb higher. Sweet birches, identified by their elliptical saw-toothed leaves, grow near the creek; we cracked open a twig and enjoyed the odor of wintergreen as we walked. Taller yellow birches push to the canopy, as do tulip poplars, oaks, and hemlocks.

Between falls, the creek provides a loquacious commentary, its mist watering thick carpets of moss and little gardens of Christmas and polypody ferns, trout lilies, and rattlesnake plantains. We spotted the stringy yellow flowers of witch hazel, bright red partridgeberries—common in fall—and the smaller but similarly red spicebush. Crushing some of the latter's berries released a refreshing smell reminiscent of lip balm. And among the forest duff we found a few fallen clusters of wild grapes—a delicious little snack that had escaped the attention of birds and other creatures. From the top overlook, we could see the upper falls and the folded hills that define the Tye River Valley. Slashing up one slope was a brigade of dead hemlocks, recently killed by the balsam wooly adelgid, presenting a vivid picture of the damage an introduced pest can inflict.

Continuing about 60 miles south on the Blue Ridge Parkway, we stopped at the Sharp Top Trail, which takes off from the Peaks of Otter Visitor Center. One of the region's greatest hikes, the trail is particularly peaceful in winter, with snow squeaking underfoot and boulders rimmed with glossy carapaces of ice. Partly paved, the trail zigzags steeply to a series of steps and, on the tip-top, along with huge lichened boulders adorning the bald peak, a pulpit of stone offers an uplifting 360-degree scan of the Piedmont, Blue Ridge, and—across the valley—the Alleghenies.

In the George Washington forest west of Staunton, Ramsey's Draft Wilderness Area embraces one of the state's largest tracts of virgin woods—some giant trees are more than 300 years old. Large hardwoods such as tulip poplar, basswood, red oak, and cucumber tree mix with hemlocks that tower over lush ferns and mosses. The draft—a local name for "creek"—runs through the middle of this wooded wilderness, freshening the air and burbling over smooth stones and big rock slabs.

In keeping with the policies of a designated wilderness, trails are minimally maintained and signs are few. A major flood in 1985 washed out portions of an old road that had made hiking up the draft relatively easy. Debris from various storms litters the trail that remains, providing more challenge to a hike that already required several fords. The resulting area is a wilder wilderness, one in which many hikers choose to go trailless, finding their way between animal trails, through thick woods, to high meadows and open views.

The Ramsey's Draft Trail starts off as a wide, easy walk on the left side of the stream. In fall, the woods flame with orange and yellow foliage against a sharp blue sky, while asters and goldenrod add color to the forest floor. The draft is wide enough for some open views of ridges even within the first mile. After a mile and a half, the trail crosses Ramsey's Draft for the second time and continues on up, following the right prong of the stream. It's about another mile and a half to a virgin stand of towering hemlocks—and a chance to get a sense of how this forest must have looked before European settlers moved into the area.

Not far south, Douthat State Park is tucked amid thousands of acres of surrounding national forestland. Easily accessible from the interstate, the park sits snug in the heart of a particularly scenic slice of the Alleghenies. One of Virginia's original half dozen state parks, Douthat showcases the work of the Civilian Conservation Corps (CCC) in the 1930s and early '40s. The detailed craftsmanship of the CCC men is still evident in the rustic lodge, restaurant, cabins, and trails, all of which helped the park achieve national historic landmark status in 1986.

The park's 25 trails explore some 43 miles of woods, passing by cascading waterfalls and climbing to open ridgetops more than 3,000 feet high. In spring the park comes to vibrant life as its dogwoods, rhododendrons, and laurels slip on lovely costumes of pink and white. Wildflowers break out from spring to autumn. In fall the hardwoods mantle themselves in the colors of the sunset—every tree from oaks and tulip poplars to dogwoods, birches, and maples gets into the act. In winter the tall hemlocks and white pines keep their greenery, while their neighbors go bare and the forest takes on a breathtaking silence. If you stand a while and listen carefully you can hear birds hunting for seeds and perhaps a deer out foraging mast along the stone cold ground. Grouse, turkey, bobcat, bear, and fox number among the other animal species that inhabit the park.

The Blue Ridge widens and rises in height the farther south it goes. Along the border with North Carolina and Tennessee, the expansive Mount Rogers National Recreation Area—slightly larger than Shenandoah National Park—pushes up into thinning air and holds rare pockets of boreal spruce-fir forest that crown Virginia's highest peaks with year-round green. High windswept meadows, kept open by grazing animals and controlled burns, have an almost alpine feel. These northern plant communities contrast richly with the lower-lying oak-hickory forests typical of the region.

Fox Creek (opposite) dodges among boulders near the Mount Rogers
Scenic Byway, while fall finery (above) clads hillsides along Route 58 east
of Grayson Highlands State Park. Typical autumn colors here in the
high country of southwestern Virginia include the golden red of sugar maples
and the bright yellows of bigtooth aspen and yellow birch.

On clear days the view from any of the recreation area's many highland balds—or meadows—is magnificent. Sterling blue mountains roar off into the southern highlands, hawks and turkey vultures soar in crystalline air, and the rounded peaks of Mount Rogers and Whitetop Mountain lift their ancient heads above the surrounding terrain. Capped by a dark green forest of Fraser fir and red spruce, these two venerable mountains are the highest in Virginia at 5,729 feet and 5,520 feet respectively. That elevation gives them the distinction of holding the state's only spruce-fir forests.

Situated about halfway between Great Smoky Mountains National Park and Shenandoah National Park, the popular Mount Rogers recreation area was carved out of the national forest in 1966 to offer travelers an alternative to those two parks. And what a wise choice. This area holds scenery, flora, and fauna unequaled anywhere in the region, with the possible exception of Shenandoah National Park. One of the most appealing aspects of the recreation area is not exactly natural. The highland balds were logged first and later converted to farmstead pastures; wild ponies and regularly scheduled prescribed fires now maintain them. These fields of grasses, rhododendrons, and blackberry bushes provide hikers wonderful open views of mountains and valleys. Though not high enough to be above tree line, the balds provide a refreshing expansive feel, especially on cool days.

Woodlands abound, too. Three wilderness areas protect more than 12,000 heavily forested acres of the recreation area. The spruce-fir forests at high elevations are often shrouded in fog and support a moist community of lush ferns, mosses, and mushrooms. Walking though this pristine northern-type ecosystem is an unusual experience so far south.

Several trails climb Mount Rogers, each providing some spectacular scenery. But be forewarned: There are no views from the forested peak itself. The highly scenic Wilburn Ridge Trail is probably the best way up, offering an exceptional walk through the spruce-fir community; it starts in Grayson Highlands State Park and makes it to the top in only a few miles. One of the greatest state parks in Virginia, Grayson Highlands soars amid the clouds and the hawks within view of Mount Rogers. High balds and exposed crags offer a number of superior mountain views within the park, while forested slopes and clear creeks provide habitat to a rich variety of wildlife. With Mount Rogers National Recreation Area on its north flank, this park offers several interesting possibilities for short and long treks.

The Cherokee used the flint they found here for tools, and they hunted wild turkey, deer, bear, and possibly buffalo. A family of settlers named Massey lived in Massie Gap in the late 19th and early 20th centuries, raising sheep and gathering ginseng and chestnuts. The gap was harvested for timber from around 1900 to 1912, then turned into pastureland. Now this big highland meadow provides wonderfully open views and serves as a nexus for several trails, including a connector to the granddaddy of them all, the Appalachian Trail, which runs through the northwest corner

Riders on the Appalachian Trail in Grayson Highlands State Park breathe in the rarified air that supports boreal plant communities.

of the park. Wild ponies keep the meadows trim, and in June rhododendron blooms splash liberal dashes of purple and white across the hillsides.

From the entrance, the park road winds about four miles up to the visitor center on Haw Orchard Mountain. At the Sugarland Overlook in fall, acres upon acres of golden red sugar maples crowd the east-facing slopes, while the Blue Ridge ripples away in the distance. Up on Massie Gap there is a broad view of a grassy bald and the compelling rise of Wilburn Ridge. The one-mile Rhododendron Trail heads up to the ridge; a bog, or seepage wetland, found about halfway up the trail, supports big Fraser firs and other northern plants. At the ridge, the Wilburn Ridge Trail takes over and ascends Mount Rogers a little more than four miles from the road.

I also like the easy Twin Pinnacles Trail behind the visitor center. It starts in an erstwhile orchard, the woods sprinkled with white-flowering hawthornes, as well as huckleberry shrubs and beech, cherry, and mountain ash trees. The hike's climax is craggy 5,089-foot Little Pinnacle, the park's highest peak. Inspiring views spread out in all directions from the summit. The mountains build in intensity toward the south, nudging into North Carolina and Tennessee. Turkey vultures, crows, and hawks arrow through the vault of sky. During fall and spring migration, red-tailed, red-shouldered, and broad-winged hawks are commonplace. This is one of the best spots anywhere for drinking in the strikingly green flanks of Mount Rogers. As I admired the view on a fall hike not too long ago, I felt thankful to live in a state blessed with such beauty. ∾

the Shenandoah

Fall leaves litter a quiet picnic spot in little-known Blue Hole Recreation Area. Tucked into a

corner of western Virginia, Blue Hole lies within the George Washington National Forest.

small gems of the Shenandoah

Mountain Lake Wilderness, a remote highland plateau in southwestern Virginia, is the largest wilderness in Jefferson National Forest. A primitive roadless area, it features a mountain bog and remnant virgin stands of hemlock and spruce set amid a gorgeous oak-hickory forest floored with azalea, mountain laurel, and blue-berry bushes. The wilderness actually lies to the northeast of Mountain Lake, one of Virginia's two natural lakes.

The cardinal flower blooms across the region in late summer.

A weathered old oak has witnessed the passing of many seasons in highland Virginia.

Buffalo Mountain Natural Area Preserve holds some of southwestern Virginia's biological treasures. The domed top of Buffalo Mountain, nearly 4,000 feet in elevation, rearing high above the surrounding countryside, receives subalpine winds and temperatures, which create a number of microhabitats that support rare plants and animals. The only place on the planet you can find Kosztarab's giant mealybug is on the outcrop barren glades near the mountaintop. Mountain sandwort, plains frostweed, and mountain rattlesnake root grow in the prairie-like communities near the summit, while red cedar–lined glades on the mountain's southern flanks hide a treasury of wildflowers and native grasses, including stiff goldenrod, purple blazing star, bog twayblade, and bog bluegrass. And grass-of-parnassus grows in the rare mafic fens—magnesium-rich groundwater seeps—found near the mountain's base.

the Alleghenies

"... deep forest-cloaked valleys carved by swift rivers ..."

A rugged land of cliff-studded mountains and wind-raked barrens, the Alleghenies of eastern West Virginia have long been an outdoor mecca for people from the stress centers of Ohio, Pennsylvania, Maryland, Virginia, and Washington, D.C. Small towns lie scattered around the deep stream-lined forests of the Alleghenies, but when you are in these woods it feels as though you could wander for days without seeing any sign of civilization. In fact, there are places in the Monongahela National Forest with some 75 contiguous square miles of vehicle-free backcountry. That's a lot of woods to get lost in. And what spectacular woods they are. As West Virginians are proud of saying: "Wild and Wonderful."

Preceding pages: Bathed in the golden light of sunset, a climber scales the face of 900-foot-high Seneca Rocks. Opposite: A small red spruce flourishes in the subarctic climate of the Dolly Sods Wilderness.

Mountain ranges of the Appalachian system, the Alleghenies march in northeast-southwest-aligned ridges from north-central Pennsylvania to southwestern Virginia; the mountains in West Virginia are the highest of the group. The Allegheny Front, or eastern continental divide, angles down the east side, separating the Allegheny Plateau from the Ridge and Valley province to the east. The South Branch of the Potomac River collects most of the water east of the front, draining into the Chesapeake Bay. Most of the water west of the front streams into the Monongahela River, which feeds into the Ohio River, which in turn rushes toward the Mississippi and the Gulf of Mexico. Throughout the region, wind and water erosion has softened the folded and faulted sedimentary rock layers.

Geography and ecology combine to make West Virginia's mountains the most biologically diverse in the Alleghenies. Deeply etched valleys hold species more common to the South, while the higher elevations support a rich component of northern plant species. Thick forests of red spruce cap the high peaks; bogs of floating sphagnum moss carpet shallow depressions; cranberries, blueberries, and wind-stunted yellow birches grow in heath barrens, often covered with snow until late spring. These boreal communities owe their existence to the last ice age, when a great ice sheet advanced as far south as Ohio, forming an immense wall of ice hundreds of feet high and blasting arctic weather to the south. When the ice began melting back, some 10,000 years ago, plant species that had migrated south continued to survive in remote high places, isolated as little islands of northern flora.

A barrier to westward travel for a long time, the Alleghenies were inevitably breached by a wave of settlers in the early 19th century, followed by railroads and highways. The railroads trundled their way into some extremely difficult terrain, down through the New River Gorge, for instance, and up over mountain passes, carrying carloads of precious coal mined from the mountains. Logging roads went even farther, poking into practically every forested cove and ridge in the region. Settlements sprang up wherever there was a valley or a hillside bench. In fact, archaeologists looking for aboriginal relics study the topography for these rare level areas, and are often rewarded with finds.

Today, the virgin hemlock, spruce, and hardwood forests are all but gone, victims of the logger's saw, yet a few hauntingly beautiful stands remain in Cathedral State Park and a few other places. In addition, luxuriant forests of oak, hickory, tulip poplar, white pine, and hemlock still blanket the hills. In spring, dogwoods, rhododendrons, azaleas, mountain laurels, and scores of wildflower species turn the understory into a riot of color and perfume. Gray foxes, raccoons, snowshoe hares, and black bears slip silently through these woods. While many animals go unobserved, bird-watchers have a good chance of seeing pileated woodpeckers, vireos, warblers, and other birds; hawks, eagles, and other raptors migrate through in the fall.

While nature lovers find much to marvel at here, river runners and rock climbers truly revere the region. The South Branch and New Rivers, and the New's tributaries,

On a rainy autumn afternoon, a white-tailed deer takes shelter beneath a serviceberry tree in the Dolly Sods, part of Monongahela National Forest.

offer any level of challenge, while Seneca Rocks ranks as one of the greatest climbing destinations in the East. And yet, this region still bristles with rough mystery, with a sense that beyond its rippling horizon there are yet more woods, more bears, more adventures—and that there are no far boundaries. In short, here is a region that can deliver any number of carry-through life memories—what more could you ask for?

The vast Monongahela National Forest of eastern West Virginia holds some of the best outdoor scenery and recreation in the Appalachians. The rugged mountain landscape varies from highland bogs and rocky outcrops to blueberry thickets and ancient spruce forests. Twisting back roads summit out to breathtaking views of deep forest-cloaked valleys carved by swift rivers, lined with steep bluffs and cliffs. In all, the forest shelters the headwaters of no less than six major rivers—the Elk, Gauley, Greenbrier, Monongahela, Potomac, and Tygart. The rivers that snake west of the Allegheny Front carry the brunt of the rainfall. The eastern slopes of the front receive half the annual precipitation of places on the west side of the front because of the rain shadow effect. Since the elevations range from 900 feet to more than 4,800 feet, moisture-ladened air coming from the west must rise to glide over the mountains. The air cools in the process and rain precipitates, leaving the leeward (east) side of the slopes drier.

the Alleghenies

Plunging six stories, brawling Blackwater Falls is audible well away from the river.

Numerous smaller, but no less dramatic, rivers thread through the mountains as well. From a thunderous 63-foot waterfall, the Blackwater River in the northern part of the forest twists and pummels its noisy way through a dramatic eight-mile-long gorge. Tannic acid from hemlock and red spruce needles stain the water its namesake dark color, actually more of an amber than true black. Situated at 3,100 feet above sea level, this remote gorge is the highlight of Blackwater Falls State Park.

A short trail ventures close enough to be sprayed by the river's furious plummet over the stony falls. In winter the falls are stacked up with ice and snow like a giant, toppling wedding cake, yet the water still manages to find a way through. On a recent winter visit here I found the snow piled thick and high, perfect for cross-country skiing, or for walking the well-packed trails. To fully appreciate the boulder-filled gorge, I laced together several short trails that allowed me to walk along its rim. Averaging about 1,000 feet wide in the park, the gorge is filled with hemlocks, maples, beeches, rhododendron, and scattered balsam firs.

Despite an abundance of rainfall, West Virginia is not known for its wetlands. In fact, the state ranks dead last, with only 1 percent of its land considered wetland. So Canaan (Ca-NANE) Valley, just south of Blackwater Falls, is a rare raft of biological diversity. Measuring 14 miles long and 2 to 4 miles wide, the oval-shaped valley is about one-third wetland. Canaan's high elevation—up to 4,300 feet—accounts for its wetness: Moist air from the west rises over the mountains, cooling and then precipitating as rain and snow. Sandwiched between Canaan Mountain on the west and Cabin Mountain on the east, Canaan Valley receives an average of 53 inches of precipitation a year. The elevation also ensures that Canaan stays relatively cold, with an average annual temperature of 44 degrees Fahrenheit and a record low of minus 24. The result is a lovely mosaic of boreal forests, meadows, and high-elevation bogs and alder swamps inhabited by beavers, minks, muskrats, ducks, and geese. Nearly one-fifth of the valley's plants are northern species, including red spruce, balsam fir, sphagnum moss, glade spurge, and highbush cranberry.

The spruce and fir communities have been here since the last ice age, when they migrated down in advance of the glaciers. These remnant boreal forests persist because of the high elevation. However, much has changed in the past two centuries. Before settlers and loggers came through, red spruces towered 90 feet tall and hemlock and birch grew in dense stands. Hoping to grow bluegrass for their livestock, farmers cleared much of the valley with fires, which ate down into the humus layer of the soil, making it hard for the spruce to regenerate. Nowadays you will find such northern hardwoods as sugar maple, yellow birch, beech, and black cherry, but only scattered stands of small spruce and fir.

The woods and wetlands support an enormous quantity of wildlife. A valuable slice of the valley is protected within Canaan Valley National Wildlife Refuge, established in 1994. To hone my birdcall and animal track identification skills, I took a guided snowshoe walk through the refuge from the White Grass Touring Center.

A weather-beaten farmhouse lends an air of old times to a pastoral Canaan Valley landscape. The valley was named in the 1700s for its likeness to the Promised Land.

Vole trails skittered across the snow and into a hole, the brush of wings perhaps indicating a predator; deer tracks disappeared into silent woods; a red-breasted nuthatch quietly stole a cone from a fir tree, while somewhere nearby a pileated woodpecker knocked for insects. Over near the refuge headquarters building, a spring-fed stream lined with heaths and sedges gurgled through a stand of aromatic balsam fir. Trees all around sported a ring of missing greenery at about waist height, a sign of browsing deer. Unfortunately, my guide informed me, this relict forest may eventually succumb to the deer and the balsam wooly adelgid insect.

My appetite whetted for more nature, I snowshoed over to the stunning highland wilderness area of Dolly Sods, which lies adjacent to Canaan Valley. (Since the roads into the Sods are unplowed, you have to get there on your own steam in winter. Another approach from the west side is to buy a one-way lift ticket at nearby Timberline, head to the top of the mountain, and ski over to Dolly Sods for some unforgettable daylong or overnight adventures. I once did this with a friend—the hard part was perching on a ski lift while wearing a fully loaded backpack.)

Dolly Sods—affectionately known just as the Sods—is a magnificent patch of high bogs and plains that covers some 10,215 acres. It draws its name from the Dahle family, who grazed sheep here in the mid-19th century on the high open plains, which they called "sods." A series of accidental fires helped keep the area open, but they burned through the soil to the rock layer, destroying the forest's ability to self-regenerate. To

Momentary master of the heights, a hiker explores the cliffs of
Bear Rocks (opposite) in the Dolly Sods Scenic Area. Situated along the
eastern continental divide, Bear Rocks gives onto the enticing barrens
and bogs of Dolly Sods (above), as well as the North Fork Valley to the east.

reestablish the woods, the forest service put in about 700 acres of red spruce and pine plantations in the 1930s. But much of the Sods remains clear and tundra-like, partly because of the extreme climate.

Here where the elevation exceeds 4,000 feet, the winds can be severe and sudden, whipping in from the west and rippling across the laurel thickets, stunting the red spruce to one-sided dwarves. Rhododendron and blueberry bushes rarely top four feet high. Yet, in any weather, the Sods is remarkable, with open views and Canadian-type flora giving hikers the distinct feeling that they've stumbled across a forgotten world, shaken loose from the far north and plopped down in West Virginia.

The Dolly Sods Scenic Area on the north end receives relatively heavy use, but the high windswept bogs and plains, punctuated with beaver ponds and grassy knolls, are wide enough to offer some solitary communion with nature, especially on weekdays in fall, winter, and spring. Flatrock Plains, a less well known backcountry area, lies in the southwest corner of the Sods. I've spent many unforgettable days and nights up here and on the adjacent Roaring Plains. Nothing but wildlands are visible in all directions, and it's easy to feel like you own the world. The mountains roll onward to the horizon, while winds roar and whistle across fields of boulders and rock slabs, dotted by patches of hardy vegetation. Hawks tilt over the plains, reading them for the little movements that spell food.

The Spruce Knob-Seneca Rocks National Recreation Area, south of Dolly Sods, is another region of rough beauty that beckons hikers. Deep forests open to clear hillsides dotted with tumbledown cabins and chimneys from 1800s homesteads. On occasion, I've ducked into some of these cabins for shelter while out hiking—the smell of old smoky wood and the sound of rain drumming a metal roof transported me to another century. The region's cool clear streams, hidden caves, and high rock walls also attract river runners and fishermen, spelunkers and rock climbers.

Named for its mists and fog, the Smoke Hole on the eastern side of the recreation area is a half-mile-deep gorge worn by the South Branch of the Potomac River as it worms its way between North Fork Mountain and Cave Mountain. Smoke Hole Road crosses the North Fork River (officially the North Fork of the South Branch of the Potomac River), then travels in the shadow of North Fork Mountain. Several trails off this road head west up to the North Fork Mountain Trail, which runs for 24 miles along the ridge of the mountain. Numerous rock outcrops and clearings among the oaks and pines give terrific views of the North Fork Valley and Alleghenies to the west; in the sky, vultures and hawks soar on updrafts.

Seneca Rocks, the signature feature in the 100,000-acre national recreation area, rises 960 exhilarating feet. The long, sharp fin of rock was made from Tuscarora sandstone laid down 400 million years ago and compacted in places to quartzite. The glorious wall once lay flat, but 275 million years ago the Appalachians began forming, buckling the Earth here to a vertical position—Seneca rests on an anticline, or upward fold, of the Earth's crust just east of the Allegheny Front. Erosion exposed and sculptured the knife-edged profile visible today.

Indians used the area as a camping ground as far back as 12,000 years ago. In fact, the field in front of the Seneca Rocks Discovery Center is a protected archaeological site holding the remains of Indian villages 600 to 800 years old. Today, rock climbers flock to Seneca to test themselves on an endless series of challenging routes with such names as Malevolence, Neck Press, and Cottonmouth. The first modern climb of the south peak was made, according to an inscription found there, in 1908. The U.S. Army's 10th Mountain Division trained here in preparation for European duty in World War II. Recreational rock climbers soon began trickling in. From personal experience, I can attest that the thrill of standing 900 feet up on a 5-foot-wide wedge of stone is hard to match this side of the Rockies.

But you don't have to be proficient with a carabiner to enjoy the excellent views from Seneca Rocks. I recently took the 1.3-mile walk from the parking lot to the observation platform nestled on the north end of the wall. Interpretive panels along the switchbacking trail explain Seneca's geology and flora, and they offer a nice pause from the 900-foot ascent. The boulders scattered along the lower section of the trail fell when ice and tree roots widened cracks in the rock above, eventually sending big chunks plummeting to the ground and adding to the talus slopes. A stunning display of such action occurred in 1987, when a 30-foot-tall piece of rock weighing 20 tons toppled, crashing into pieces. The vegetation along the trail changes as the trail ascends and the soil thins. At the lower elevations, flowers such as jack-in-the-pulpit grow in moist, shady areas; higher up, lichens, laurels, and table mountain pines find niches in drier conditions. The overlook at trail's end faces west toward the Allegheny Plateau. Seneca Creek carves down the mountain out front, sheep and cattle pastures green the hillsides all around, and the barks of farm dogs rise from far below.

The national recreation area's other focal point is 4,863-foot Spruce Knob, the highest peak in West Virginia. The peak rises at the south end of Spruce Mountain, a 12-mile-long ridge running northeast. A steep and winding 12-mile road with few guardrails, but lots of scenic overlooks, climbs toward the summit. An observation tower on the top rewards determined motorists and hikers with sweeping panoramas of grassy pastures and forested mountains.

The half-mile Whispering Spruce Trail that circles the summit offers a close look at the knob's high-country vegetation. The winds and temperatures up here can be severe, pruning the hardy red spruce and mountain ash to a krummholz forest of chest-high, gnarled trees, some of them wearing thick vegetation low to the ground and others taking a flag shape—flag spruce have a webbing of dead branches to windward, protecting the greenery on the other side, similar to wind-pruned trees on the Outer Banks.

the Alleghenies

Delicate looking, but hardy survivors, marsh marigolds (above) and other
plants in Cranberry Glades Botanical Area migrated south with the Ice Age and
remain in high pockets of cold air and boggy soil. Tender curled shoots of
skunk cabbage (opposite) emerge in spring; when bruised, the plant releases
a foul odor of decaying meat that attracts pollinating insects.

Located in the southern part of Monongahela National Forest, Cranberry Glades is another of the handful of places in West Virginia that has remnant boreal plant communities from the Ice Age. But none have as extensive an area of open glades as Cranberry. Limned by dark-green borders of deliciously aromatic spruce and hemlock, the four bogs here spread out in unexpected gardens of northern flora.

Mats of decaying sphagnum moss form a spongy layer of peat more than 12 feet thick that composes the floor of an acidic wetland. These bogs, or muskegs as they are called in the far north, support carnivorous sundews, sedges, orchids, mosses, and other plants that can tolerate the acidic soil and cold climate.

The Cranberry Glades Boardwalk offers a delightful, short educational stroll across two of the bogs, starting in a forest of shallow-rooted yellow birch, hemlock, and red spruce, then emerging in an open glade. My children had great fun making one discovery after another here. A wide carpet of wet sphagnum moss is leavened with ferns and the small vines of cranberries—in summer tiny pinkish white flowers bloom, followed by the dark red berries. Haircap moss, reindeer moss, and bog rosemary are among the many other plants growing here. Swaths of cotton grass bloom in white puffs in late summer, and skunk cabbage wafts its foul odor in nearby thickets of shrubby spotted alder, attracting insects. Sprouting rapidly and as early as February, skunk cabbage can melt snow with the heat of its cellular respiration. A bruised-looking green and purple-brown spathe covers the tiny flowers, which give way to huge cabbage-like leaves. The boardwalk crosses Yew Creek, which waters a strip of bog forest, then heads around to Flag Glade, where in early summer you may see tiny sundews and a number of orchids, including the delicate violet-tinged rose pogonia.

Spreading north of the botanical area are the contiguous 35,864-acre Cranberry Wilderness and 26,000-acre Cranberry Back Country, together forming a vast tract of formerly cutover forest that rises to more than 4,600 feet in elevation. Motorized vehicles are not allowed in the backcountry; the wilderness goes a step further by not even allowing bicycles. What you have here is about 75 square miles of wildlife-filled, stream-riven, wild country for exploring on foot and skis. Motorists can explore the edges of this vast area on the 45-mile Highland Scenic Highway; it begins along the winding North Fork of the Cherry River, then shoots north up State Route 150. Overlooks of Cranberry Glades and the surrounding ridges and valleys offer a bird's-eye view—breezes corkscrew through the high grasses, ruffling them into changing textures and patterns.

The Cherokee called the nearby wide, shallow Greenbrier River Watauga, "the river of islands." For several miles the river winds along the borders of West Virginia's largest state park, swashing around little islands and sandbars. Cloaked in a dense forest of hardwoods and hemlocks, Watoga State Park is bordered by more woodlands—Calvin Price State Forest on the south and Monongahela National

Monongahela wilderness areas

A few wildernesses in the Monongahela warrant special mention. The lovely 20,000-acre Otter Creek Wilderness north of Alpena harbors black bears, snow-shoe hares, and white-tailed deer in its heavy forest, which varies from native red spruce and planted Norway spruce in the high elevations to black cherry, yellow birch, and other hardwoods lower down. In keeping with a designated wilderness, trails are unmarked and minimally maintained. Hikers follow ridges and streambeds, though in places the rhododendron and laurel thickets make the going impossible. Flash floods are common during heavy rains, as streams course into the natural bowl formed by Shavers and McGowan Mountains. In the early 1970s, hikers and hunters joined ranks to ban logging and dirt biking from the area and turn it into a wilderness; Congress designated it as such in 1975.

Southeast of Glady, the less well known Laurel Fork North and South Wildernesses cover 12,052 acres and share with Otter Creek a history of logging and burning. Since 1983, both areas have been left to revert to their natural state; however, the timber management from the 1960s has resulted in some strikingly open, high-ceilinged forests of tall straight trees—including beech, cherry, maple, birch, and tulip poplar. Now deer, wild turkey, bobcat, and beaver make homes here.

Cranberry creepers entwine a mat of sphagnum moss.

High cotton in Cranberry Glades: Growing up to four feet tall, tawny cotton grass thrives in a

glade bordered by red spruce. Cotton grass is actually a sedge, or tufted marsh plant.

Forest on the east and north. White-tailed deer abound in these hilly woods, as do black bears, gray foxes, wild turkeys, raccoons, and woodchucks. In winter, snows sugar the hemlocks and rhododendrons and ice edges in on the lake and streams, giving the park a fairyland look.

Mountain laurel and rhododendron flourish along trails that loop through woods and clearings. More trails course through the park's Brooks Arboretum, which holds a huge variety of native trees and shrubs: tulip tree, hemlock, red maple, beech, river birch, black gum, black cherry, serviceberry, dogwood, oak, and hickory, to name but a few. Also growing here are saplings of American chestnuts. Though the great chestnut forests were wiped out by blight in the 1930s, their progeny grows from old stumps, sometimes reaching 20 feet before succumbing to the fungus.

The southern part of the park has been left undeveloped; only a few trails and old logging roads venture into this wildlife haven. The Arrowhead Trail, one of the most rewarding trails in the park, begins at the riverside campground and makes a steep one-mile ascent to a lookout tower. About halfway up on one hike I saw turkey scratchings on the ground, then heard rustling in the thickets of rhododendron; pretty soon I saw the birds themselves flapping quickly out of the way. Woodpeckers called with a raucous *queet queet queet* and rapped their beaks high in the treetops, while deer scampered for cover. The sound of the ruffed grouse slapping his wings together to attract a mate echoed in the woods. On top of the ridge, huckleberry and wild phlox grew in profusion in a clearing. From the two-story lookout tower I had a wonderful westward view of the mountains and farmlands, while down below the Greenbrier River rushed along its course.

The New River writhes its way north from North Carolina over the rugged Appalachian Plateau, carving out a dramatic gorge some 1,600 feet deep and 3,000 feet wide in southern West Virginia. Flanking 53 miles of this stretch of the river, the long and sinuous New River Gorge National River is a haven for white-water enthusiasts and fishermen, and it has allowed the forest to reclaim coal mining towns and sites that flourished from the 1870s to the early 1950s.

The New was once part of the ancient Teays River system that flowed north through West Virginia and across central Ohio, Indiana, and Illinois, draining all of the east-central United States. During the last ice age, glaciers pushed far enough south to obliterate the Teays's course; the part of the river that meandered across West Virginia swelled up into a 200-mile-long lake. The lake eventually overflowed, but since a glacial dam blocked its northward journey, it formed a new channel, known today as the Ohio River. The upper portion of the Teays, rising from near Blowing Rock, North Carolina, is now known as the New River, even though it more or less follows its original route. No one knows exactly how old the New River is. Estimates vary from 3 to 320 million years old, depending upon how the river's age is measured.

A fan of canoes awaits river runners at a Greenbrier River outfitter. The Greenbrier watershed hosts a variety of life, from freshwater mussels to great blue herons.

One calculation for major U.S. rivers approximates 6,000 years for every foot of gorge depth—at 1,600 feet deep, the age would be about 10 million years. But the New River Gorge is only one-third as deep as the Grand Canyon, which is 5 to 10 million years old; using this gauge, the New may only be 2 to 3 million years old. Many experts, however, believe the New River began cutting its gorge after the last Appalachian uplift, making its age about 65 million years. If so, the New would be one of the oldest rivers on Earth.

The river drops 750 feet on its 50-mile run from the Bluestone Dam to the Gauley Bridge, generating rapids up to Class V in intensity. At the Gauley Bridge, the river becomes the Kanawha, which flows north into the Ohio. Tilted rock layers are exposed along the gorge, its depth diminishing toward the north as the surrounding ridges lower in elevation. The layers, originally sand, mud, trees, and plants, compacted over millions of years into sandstone, shale, and coal—about 50 feet of vegetation for every foot of coal. The sandstone cliffs are obvious to the visitor. Not so obvious are the deposits of coal that rapidly altered the landscape in the 19th and 20th centuries. When the New River Gorge was linked to the Ohio River by railroad in 1873, dozens of little coal mining towns sprang up along the river. Until the end of World War II, the mining and timber industries operated full steam.

It's hard to believe how busy the gorge was then. Thousands of people lived between Thurmond and Fayette Station in the north part of the gorge. Sawmills

the Alleghenies

Weekend rafters get a taste of the turbulent Gauley River. Water from the Summersville Dam

is released on fall weekends, generating monster rapids and big profits for local businesses.

Spanning more than half a mile, the single-arch New River Gorge Bridge shoots over the 900-foot-deep canyon of the New River.

buzzed; coke ovens blasted out sulphurous vapors; trains rattled along the river, belching smoke; saloons, dance halls, and brothels did a brisk business in the shadow of numerous schools and churches. Today, coal tipples lie rusting, snared by vines and trees. Wood rats nest in the crumbling ruins of coke ovens, while deer browse the leafy plants growing from the foundations of old houses and princess trees bloom purple on abandoned hillsides. Goldenrod, gama grass, and trumpet creeper have found niches in a wasteland. Bit by bit, clearings are giving way to forest, and the forest is maturing to something approaching its former glory.

Down along tributary streams, willows and sweet gums grow in a moist riparian habitat. Beavers build dams along here, and salamanders feast on crayfish and insects. Higher, on the upland slopes, hickory, birch, sassafras, and black gum hold sway over a festival of blooming azaleas, Indian pipes, trout lilies, lady's slippers, and serviceberries. Bobcats, raccoons, and a few black bears lead stealthy nocturnal lives in this zone. Way up on the rocky rim, oaks and pines can take the drier, windier conditions; such heaths as huckleberry and blueberry grow in the understory. White-tailed deer often frequent these parts. Winding the updrafts above the gorge are turkey vultures, hawks, falcons, and even eagles and ospreys.

The view south into the V-shaped gorge from the boardwalk at the Canyon Rim Visitor Center showcases the area's finery, its forested slopes disappearing in the misty distance. Nine hundred feet below, the river runs swiftly; its tumult is just a sibilant whisper up here. The forces of nature are evident all around; so, too, is the force of man. The New River Gorge Bridge stands in testimony to man's desire to conquer nature. It was built in 1977 to supercede the iron truss bridge down below. The old bridge makes a short hop over the river; the new one leaps 3,031 feet across the entire canyon, cutting the rim-to-rim commute from a zigzagging 40 minutes to a straight shot of less than 1 minute. The new link is considered the second longest single-arch steel bridge in the world.

As spectacular as the panoramas are from Canyon Rim, Grandview farther upriver offers still more thrills. A state park until being absorbed into the national river park in 1990, Grandview stands more than 1,400 feet above a Z-curve in the river. The main overlook lies a short stroll from the parking lot and takes in a stunning sweep of river and gorge. The trail itself is quite fantastic: It hugs the base of sandstone cliffs that stand stacked up to 75 feet high and overhang far enough in places to shelter the path from the elements. Virgin's bower, fox grape, bittersweet, poison ivy, Virginia creeper, and other vines creep along the trail or up the cliffs. In autumn, the blooms of ironweed, goldenrods, and asters provide brilliant splashes of color; come wintertime, organ pipes of ice hang from the cliffs, and the white snow makes a brilliant contrast with the vivid greens of rhododendron, hemlock, and moss. Bare trees reveal a network of logging roads on the mountains across the river.

Down below, the river churns. Several miles upriver, Sandstone Falls makes an impressive 10- to 25-foot drop where the river measures 1,500 feet across. Thought to have been a sandbar in a sea 300 million years ago, these are the largest falls on the river. An overlook on the east side of State Route 20 offers a fabulous view from high up. In winter, the river is frostbitten with white floes, yet the falls still thunder.

To many people, the New River is synonymous with white water. From Hinton to Thurmond, the river makes a long, looping calligraphic line, punctuated with Class I to Class III falls; only at Brooks and Sandstone is a portage necessary. Below Thurmond, however, the river becomes a demonic Mr. Hyde of tumultuous rapids, ranging up to Class V. The best season for river running is April to June, though the entire river can be run through fall. A day or two spent paddling the river offers a book's worth of perspective on the gorge's natural history. River runners seeking more of a challenge head for the Gauley River National Recreation Area. The Gauley joins the New north of Canyon Rim. Dam releases in the fall turn the steep, narrow Gauley into a treacherous waterway, studded with more than 100 rapids within 25 miles. Only expert rafters, kayakers, and canoeists dare take on the huge boulders and hydraulics of this river.

But the thrill of breathtaking scenery is plenty satisfying in itself. And this region excels at wild and wonderful scenery. From the Blackwater to the New River, the natural features of West Virginia's Alleghenies owe their presence to the power of water. Water over time equals rare beauty. ✑

Fully operational, picturesque Glade Creek Grist Mill sells its own products to park visitors.

Babcock State Park centers on a steep Y-shaped gorge slashed by two swift streams, Manns Creek and Glade Creek. One of the park's highlights, a trail skirts the rim of a 1,100-foot-deep, boulder-lined canyon, offering wonderful mountain views. At the base of one headland lies a cave that reputedly served as a hideout for a gang of robbers who once preyed on the payroll trains that chugged along the area's narrow-gauge logging railways.

Twenty miles of trails wind through scenic woodlands, which in June are rife with the blooms of rhododendrons, particularly the purple Catawba and the white maximum, the state flower.

The park's working Glade Creek Grist Mill, completed in 1976, was built from parts of three West Virginia gristmills, some more than a century old. Standing near the site of an earlier mill, the present one serves as a vivid reminder of the 500 working mills that once dotted the state.

small gems of the Alleghenies

Cranesville Swamp: When the Ice Age glaciers pushed refrigerated air into the Southern Appalachians, they created ecosystems with cold-adapted plants such as Canada yew, red spruce, and cranberry. After the glaciers' retreat some 10,000 years ago, a few pockets of sub-arctic life were left in little microclimates that had the right combination of cold and moisture to support this lush variety of northern flora. Situated in a mountain valley at 2,900 feet, Cranesville Swamp on the border of West Virginia and Maryland is such an example.

The spongy peat bog here is perfectly suited for sphagnum moss, the carnivorous sundew, club moss, skunk cabbage, and others—in total some 200 plant species. An adjoining forest of eastern hemlock, spruce, red maple, white pine, yellow birch, quaking aspen, and tamarack grows just beyond the nutrient-poor soil of the bog. The tamaracks, or eastern larches, that grow here are the southernmost in the United States.

Daylight fades on pines and tamaracks in Cranesville Swamp.

the Smokies

"... a seemingly endless ocean of blue mountains."

The Appalachians reach their crescendo in North Carolina and Tennessee. Nowhere else in the entire 2,000-mile Newfoundland-to-Alabama chain do the mountains rise so high. You'd have to go all the way to western South Dakota, practically into Wyoming, to achieve such elevation on land. North Carolina alone contains 82 peaks more than 5,000 feet high—and 43 of these top 6,000 feet. The air is noticeably thinner and cooler on the highest peaks, contributing to a sensation of more western or northern ecology. Among the many ranges, the Great Smoky Mountains are perhaps the best known because of the national park, but numerous other ranges offer similar opportunities for exploring the southern Appalachian landscape.

Preceding pages: Above the clouds, the high ridges of the Appalachians rise and fall like mythical monsters in an ancient sea. Opposite: Sunrise silhouettes a spruce on Clingmans Dome, the highest point in Great Smoky Mountains National Park.

Though the North Carolina and Tennessee mountains are the highest in the Appalachians, they are mere remnants of what they once were. It all started about a billion years ago, when periods of sedimentation and eruption created such high heat and pressure that rocks metamorphosed—clayey shales into slate and schist, magma into granite, and sandstone into quartzite. The pressure cooker these Precambrian rocks endured was so intense that no fossils are found in them today. The rocks are exposed as cliffs and pinnacles around the region. After attaining nearly Himalayan heights, the Appalachians began slowly wearing down. Periods of freezing helped split big chunks of stone from high cliffs; streams and rivers carved and carved away, washing mighty mountains to the sea. Eventually, perhaps millions of years from now, this mountain chain—one of the oldest on Earth—will crumble to a few hills, then a level plain.

Meanwhile, the rugged southern Appalachians continue on into a distinguished old age. They divide in this region into two major northeast-southwest-aligned ranges—the Blue Ridge on the east and the Unakas on the Tennessee–North Carolina border. Instead of a valley between these two ranges, there are ridges spanning the gap, creating a complex jumble of peaks. When you stand on a high point in the middle of the region—a memorable experience—you are surrounded by a seemingly endless ocean of blue mountains. One of the cross ridges contains the Black Mountain group, home to 6,684-foot Mount Mitchell and 6,647-foot Mount Craig, the highest mountains in the East.

One of the most interesting phenomena of the region is its teeming variety of plant life. After the last ice age, some 10,000 years ago, many northern plant species retreated to higher elevations. Canadian spruce-fir forests now grow atop the cool highlands of the southern Appalachians, while farther downslope grow hickory, poplar, and oak—all in all the most extensive broad-leaved deciduous forest in the world. Furthermore, the high mountains function as a rain catcher, trapping warm moist air from the south and turning it into heavy precipitation; the result is a lush forest holding many record-size trees.

Beneath the canopy, redbud, serviceberry, laurel, dogwood, and other trees flower in gaudy shades of purple, white, yellow, and pink. Spring through fall, hundreds of species of wildflowers carpet the forest floor. Black bears, deer, European boars, wild turkeys, and migrating warblers are but a few of the animals that take advantage of the coves, valleys, and high ridges. Though the area remains sparsely populated by people, visitors stream in for shows of spring flowers and autumn leaves.

A vast treasury of forested highlands, Pisgah National Forest in North Carolina sprawls over nearly 800 square miles of the Unaka and Blue Ridge mountain chains, encompassing hundreds of miles of trails and some 120 miles of the scenic Blue Ridge Parkway. Within the forest's two segments are 20 peaks topping 6,000 feet, including

In Moses H. Cone Memorial Park off the Blue Ridge Parkway,
riders enjoy some of the 25 miles of carriage trails.

Mount Mitchell. The famous Appalachian Trail skirts Pisgah's northwest boundary, and 79 miles of the Forest Heritage National Scenic Byway (U.S. 276 and State Route 215) run through the forest between Brevard and Waynesville. Throughout the forest, there are thundering waterfalls, towering rock cliffs, and breathtaking mountaintop views

The oldest of the state's four national forests, Pisgah dates its origins to 1911, when the Weeks Act authorized the U.S. government to purchase lands to be set aside as national forests. That year the government bought an 8,100-acre tract south of Mount Mitchell. About three years later, the widow of industrialist George Vanderbilt sold the government a 78,410-acre parcel of land around Mount Pisgah, which had been part of the original Biltmore estate. From these first two holdings, the Pisgah—established in 1916, and the first national forest in the East—grew to its present size. Combined with the adjoining 531,000-acre Nantahala National Forest just south and the 640,000-acre Cherokee National Forest in Tennessee, the Pisgah holds a tremendous portion of the remaining southern Appalachian forest.

Despite its commercial fanfare, privately owned Grandfather Mountain, at the northern end of the Pisgah, is well worth the price of admission for its stunning views, network of trails, and mile-high swinging bridge. The rough-cut 5,964-foot peak was named by early settlers for the bearded-patriarch profile visible from the north. The Cherokee called it Tanawha, meaning "hawk" or "eagle." In the fall, broad-winged hawks migrate through the area and make an especially thrilling sight from the naked ramparts of this rugged mountain.

the Smokies

Catching the last rays of day, the giant eye of Looking Glass Rock in Pisgah National Forest

gleams in lonely splendor. Rock climbers love the slick face of the 3,969-foot-high dome.

The grassy bald of 4,629-foot-high Max Patch in Pisgah National Forest offers a view of the blue foothills of the Smokies.

So tall and imposing is Grandfather Mountain that it was once thought to be the highest peak in the East. It turns out, though, that it is only the highest point in the Blue Ridge. Erosion-resistant quartzite, exposed after an older rock layer wore away millions of years ago, makes up the bulk of the massif. About 20 kinds of rare plants shelter in Grandfather's varied habitats, among them balsam groundsel and pink-shelled azalea. Birches grow in the lower moist areas of the mountain, while tangles of blackberry and blueberry coil along the edges of heath balds on the mountainsides; higher up, blankets of diminutive spruce and fir hunker against severe winter weather. Dark gray outcrops offer excellent vantage points for long views of mountains and ridges and for studying soaring birds.

To the south, Pisgah's Linville Gorge ranks as one of the most pristine and magnificent wilderness areas in the southern Appalachians. Dropping from high on Grandfather Mountain, the Linville River gains momentum as it slashes down through the towering quartzite walls of the gorge. Over the millennia, the river has chiseled a spectacular 12-mile-long chasm of twisting rapids, deep pools, and craggy cliffs more than 600 feet high.

Popular Linville Falls lies just off the Blue Ridge Parkway at mile 316. Several trails meander along the river to overlooks of the falls and plunge basins. A tremendous volume of water gushes from the 50-foot upper falls into a huge rectangular basin, then plummets from a cut in the rock another 60 feet to the lower falls. All around are awe-inspiring high walls, stone towers, and the constant washing rhythm of the river.

The wild and beautiful Linville Gorge Wilderness was designated in 1964, making it one of the first two wilderness areas in the East—the other, the Shining Rock Wilderness, also in Pisgah, lies southwest of Asheville. Falling some 2,000 feet in 12 miles, Linville River passes through several plant communities and vast tracts of virgin forest. The ubiquitous rosebay rhododendron grows in thickets on rocky slopes and ridges, frustrating many a hiker who attempts to bushwhack in these parts. The rhododendron, the sourwood, and the pink-blooming mountain laurel all belong to the hardy heath family and take root in "laurel slicks"—a colloquialism for dense thickets—or under high canopy.

Continuing south, several transverse ranges bridge the northeast-southwest lie of the Appalachians. The Black Mountains, the Craggies, the Pisgahs, and the Balsams link the greater chains like rungs and create an endless sea of peaks and valleys. The Crabtree Meadows Recreation Area (parkway mile 339), in the shadow of the hulking Black Mountains, makes for a delightful respite, especially in May with the pink mountain laurel at full bloom, and the forest floor littered with jack-in-the-pulpits, lady's slippers, and showy orchises.

Mount Mitchell—the highest peak east of South Dakota's Black Hills—belongs to the short but lofty Black Mountains chain. In a mere 15 miles, the range holds seven of the ten highest peaks in the East. For many years, Grandfather Mountain was presumed the highest point in the region and New Hampshire's Mount Washington the highest in the East, but in 1835, Dr. Elisha Mitchell, a science professor from the University of North Carolina, trekked into the area to settle the question once and for all. He believed the Black Mountains to be the highest in the East and his calculations, based on barometric pressure readings on three visits, proved his point. Mitchell showed that this peak is more than 700 feet higher than Grandfather and almost 400 feet higher than Mount Washington. One of his estimates was only 12 feet short of the official height of 6,684 feet recognized today. In 1857, when a former student disputed his claim, Mitchell went back to the mountains with his instruments. He fell from a 40-foot cliff over a waterfall to his death. The following year the mountain was named for him; he lies buried on the peak.

With a tremendous surge in logging in the 1910s, locals began speaking up for the forest, and in 1915 Mount Mitchell became North Carolina's first state park. The air atop Mount Mitchell is so thin and cool, you'd think you were in southern Canada. The plants and animals certainly do—the microclimate here supports life rarely seen anywhere else in the South. It would be nice to report that the forest on the peak is healthy today; unfortunately, a tiny insect called the balsam woolly adelgid is killing many of the Fraser firs. Since the spruces are also dying, scientists speculate that acid rain and low-level ozone have a lot to do with the tree decline as well. And it does not help that ice storms and strong winds, often in excess of

100 miles an hour, prune out trees that would normally be strong enough to survive. However, the views from the top on clear days are still among the greatest anywhere in the nation. The 30-foot observation tower on the peak rides atop a world of blue-green mountains—distant peaks pop up on the circular horizon up to 90 miles away like little puffs of smoke. Grandfather Mountain is a smudge of aqua paint 35 miles to the northeast.

Pisgah National Forest has more sights to stir the soul southwest of Asheville. The forest's 155,000-acre Pisgah District began as managed woodlands on the Biltmore estate at the turn of the 20th century. Vanderbilt's head forester, Dr. Carl A. Schenck, spent time and money in cutting timber, replanting trees, and stocking deer, turkey, and trout, practices he learned in his native Germany. His way, it turns out, was the right way, and it has paid off in a healthy forest and watershed, brimming with wildlife and native plant species.

Among more than 350 miles of trails in the Pisgah District, the 16-mile Shut-in Trail crosses some of the most outstanding scenery in the Blue Ridge. Starting with an overlook of the French Broad River, the strenuous trail follows the ridge southwest along an old horse trail used by Vanderbilt to get to a hunting lodge. The trail pierces dense tunnels of laurel and rhododendron, steps out onto bald knobs, and ends with a stirring view of the domed top of 5,721-foot Mount Pisgah, named by a Scotch-Irish Presbyterian minister for the mountain upon which Moses spotted the Promised Land.

Finally, nearby Looking Glass Rock is one of the largest granite monoliths in the southern Appalachians. Shooting up impressively from the surrounding forest, the domed face has long been a magnet to rock climbers. I made my first ascent as a teenager. Now, nearly 30 years later, I'm content with the trails along the base. After a invigorating hike, or climb, it is a delight to take to the water at Sliding Rock in Looking Glass Creek; sliding over smooth rock into the plunge pool has a way of making you feel young again.

Just over the Tennessee border, Roan Mountain State Park is a natural jewel, as well as a good base for a visit to the rhododendron gardens on top of the mountain. Snuggled into the north side of the 6,285-foot peak of Roan Mountain, the verdant park has many enticements—more than 180 species of wildflowers, 15 miles of trails, and a great variety of songbirds and other wildlife.

One local story claims that Daniel Boone visited the mountain on a roan horse, for which the mountain was then named. Another legend has it that the name stems from the roan or dark red color of the mountain's flora—rhododendrons in June, ash berries in September. Among 18th- and 19th-century botanists to study the mountain were André Michaux, John Fraser, and Asa Gray; they reported on such new plants as the Catawba rhododendron, Fraser fir, and Gray's lily.

Plunge pools, lower falls, and stone towers of Linville Falls prove nature a master landscaper.

Long-distance hikers relish the sweeping views afforded by the Round Bald section of the Appalachian Trail above Roan Mountain State Park.

The area's general appeal dates back at least as far as 1877, when Gen. Thomas Wilder built a 20-room inn on the top of Roan Mountain. Business was so good that in 1885 he replaced the inn with the 166-room Cloudland Hotel; visitors patient enough to endure a long jolting carriage ride over the narrow trail to the summit were rewarded with grand views of the rhododendrons and the surrounding mountains. Wilder also had bought 7,000 acres of area land, which he mined for iron ore. By 1900, most of the ore was gone, and so was Wilder—he sold out and moved on. The hotel was abandoned, then taken apart. The mature balsam (Fraser) fir and red spruce were felled, and even the rhododendrons were dug out and sold to nurseries. By 1939, just about all the saleable timber had been picked over.

But nature found a way to come back. The natural rhododendron gardens revived and the surrounding spruce and Fraser fir were kept in check by the U.S. Forest Service. Today, the gardens are part of Pisgah National Forest. Though the park and the base of the mountain lie in Tennessee, the gardens at the top are just over the line in North Carolina.

From the park entrance, it is a ten-mile drive to the top of the mountain. Grassy balds and heath gardens punctuate the almost four-mile ridgeline between the gap and Roan High Bluff; the mountain's high point is Roan High Knob. The balds possibly started with the grazing of prehistoric animals, then were maintained by elk and bison and, later, by sheep, cows, horses, goats, and pigs.

Visitors in mid-June are treated to the sight and scent of 600 acres of rhododendron in full red and purple glory. But at any time of year, the area is a rare gift. The elevation provides cool air on the hottest days, and the stands of sturdy little spruce and hemlock offer their own gardens of mosses and ferns and wildflowers. Trails loop through the natural gardens, pausing here and there at overlooks for distant views of the rippling smoky blue mountains to the south. One sweet trail ends at Roan High Bluff for a spectacular bird's-eye vista of long, low mountains to the west and the green valley around the little town of Buladean, North Carolina, down below.

Spread across ten counties, the flora and fauna of Cherokee National Forest form part of an extensive system of southern Appalachian woodlands that extends into the Carolinas and Georgia. Thick carpets of poplar, oak, hemlock, and pine roll over the mountainous geography, interrupted by deep ravines, cool streams, and tumbling waterfalls. Above 5,000 feet grow forests of small spruce and fir. Also on high mountaintops, rhododendron gardens and grassy balds flourish, creating microhabitats where both northern and southern plant species live. Other specialized niches are created around rock outcrops, beech-maple woods, mountain bogs, the sprayed cliffs of waterfalls, streamside forests, and the backed-up water in beaver ponds. In fact, these special communities, though they account for only a small portion of the forest acreage, hold about 75 percent of Cherokee's rare plant and animal species.

In the springtime, the lilting songs of warblers and vireos ring throughout the forest as the birds arrive from farther south and begin setting up house for the summer. Dogwood and redbud trees burst into bloom, and bouquets of trout lilies, wild geraniums, dwarf crested irises, and bluets lie strewn across the forest floor. Summer brings out the rhododendrons and a host of flowers; hummingbirds sip on jewelweed and bee balm; broad-winged hawks and other raptors cruise high overhead; and black bears find mates and enjoy long days filled with blackberries and blueberries. With the return of autumn, dogwood, maple, sweetgum, and sourwood deck the hillsides in tones of gold and russet; white-tailed deer are in rut; and hibernating animals work long days gathering food. In the cold, hard frosts of January, bear cubs are born in warm dens, and by late February maples and spicebushes brave the chill with swelling buds.

East of Greeneville, Tennessee, in the heart of the Nolichucky/Unaka Ranger District, the limpid Paint Creek courses through hardwood coves, spills over mossy waterslides, and joins with the picturesque French Broad River. Maple and blackgums flame scarlet in the creek's corridor in fall, and in early spring the blooms of the trailing arbutus, bloodroot, and crimson fire pink litter the ground. Year-round, hemlocks tower overhead and the air is tinged with the fresh scent of pine. The soft murmur of the creek rises to a roar as it falls over the high overhanging cliff known as

Rainy, foggy days bring out the beauty of close-up views, such as

the vibrant autumn colors of these maple leaves in Cherokee National Forest.

Painted Rock. Here the creek empties into the French Broad River, a wide river that flows northwest. The 107-foot-high rock face is decorated with the graffiti of generations of soldiers and travelers. Native Americans made pictographs on the wall. This quiet bend in the forest held a Federal blockhouse in 1794, then a post office and general store, past which drovers herded livestock between Greeneville, Tennessee, and Greenville, South Carolina.

On a recent trip here I walked down to the broad rocky beach on the river and savored the present-day peace and quiet. Then I climbed Painted Rock and was extremely grateful that I took my time—I was suddenly on top, staring down a sheer drop-off. From here there are great views up and down the river, which envelops islands and passes by low hills.

The Cherokee called the forbiddingly rugged southwest corner of North Carolina Nantahala—"land of the noonday sun"—because its gorges were so deep the sun could reach them only at midday. Today the Nantahala National Forest, the largest in the state, covers much of that same lushly forested, mountainous countryside. Nantahala's dozens of rivers, three wilderness areas, scores of waterfalls, and miles of trails make this a good place to lose yourself in.

Here on the Blue Ridge escarpment, the mountains make a precipitous drop to the Piedmont plain, leaving a legacy of glorious waterfalls. Many waterfalls are claimed to be the highest in the East, depending upon how they are measured. Certainly the Whitewater Falls, a thrilling series of Whitewater River cascades totaling 411 vertical feet, are among the highest and most beautiful. Just across the South Carolina state line, the Lower Whitewater Falls make a similarly impressive 400-foot descent.

The Chattooga River originates not far north on 4,930-foot Whiteside Mountain, south of the town of Cashiers. Rising 2,100 feet from the valley, the green-mantled monarch is flanked by spectacular granitic gneiss cliffs that soar from 400 to 750 feet sheer. The two-mile Whiteside Mountain Trail climbs to the top of the mountain, allowing ample time for studying the scenery close up and far away. Traveling through a forest of red oaks, Fraser magnolias, and black birches, the pathway is sprinkled with white wood asters, blueberries, wild sarsaparilla, and the fall-flowering witch hazel. From the top are splendid views to the east, west, and south. In spring and summer, peregrine falcons, reintroduced here in 1985, return to nest.

The 2,000-foot-deep Nantahala Gorge, a must-see area of the forest, parallels U.S. 19, the Mountain Waters National Scenic Byway. This turbulent nine-mile stretch of the Nantahala River offers rafters and kayakers world-class river running as the water crashes around boulders and forms raft-swamping waves on its rush north to Fontana Lake. It is not all natural—the water is controlled by releases from the dam on Nantahala Lake—but when you are on the river it looks plenty wild. I once made it down in a kayak without capsizing, and felt I had accomplished something.

The most untouched area of the forest lies in the northwest, where the 3,800-acre Joyce Kilmer Memorial Forest harbors a magnificent stand of old-growth poplars, hemlocks, and oaks, several nearly four centuries old and measuring more than 20 feet around and 100 feet tall. Walking in this shadowy forest of giants—the largest parcel of old growth in the East—is a rare privilege. In spring, giant chickweeds, Canadian violets, and trout lilies knit a light counterpoint to the tall trees. The adjoining Joyce Kilmer–Slickrock Wilderness, and Citico Creek Wilderness in Tennessee's Cherokee National Forest, protect a further 33,300 acres, sheltering bear, deer, bobcat, and other wildlife.

If you stand atop Clingmans Dome on a crisp morning, the world rolls out in front of you for 50 miles or more in all directions. Low-lying rafts of clouds create burly island continents out of blue-gray mountain ranges, lit on their eastern flanks by the rising sun. Up on the highest point of the Great Smokies, it is easy to see why a park was created here. In addition to its incomparable beauty, the park boasts more than 30 forested peaks topping 5,000 feet, 16 of these more than 6,000 feet high.

Great Smoky Mountains National Park ranks as the most heavily visited national park in the country; it is also one of the largest protected areas east of the Rockies, containing some of the East's biggest tracts of virgin forest. Perhaps most important, though, the park holds a mind boggling biological diversity: more than 5,500 known species of plants, 60 native mammal species, 200 bird species, 38 kinds of reptiles, 41 kinds of amphibians, and 58 species of fish. Designated an international biosphere reserve, the park likely has the richest biological mix of any place on the continent.

The Smokies occupy the widest part of the Unakas, the mountains that run parallel to and west of the Blue Ridge. They are composed primarily of sedimentary rock laid down about 50,000 feet thick more than 600 million years ago. After various episodes of folding and faulting, the rock layers were pushed into tremendous mountains. Relentless water, wind, rain, and ice eroded the surface, cutting valleys between the ridges. The Ice Age glaciers of 500,000 to 20,000 years ago never reached this point, but the extreme periods of freezing and thawing left their marks. Tremendous boulders cracked loose from cliffs and thundered down into creekbeds, where they lie today. Cold-adapted plants migrated to higher elevations, leaving them cut off from their northern population base. Southern species filled in the valleys, and a uniquely variegated plant community was born.

The Great Smoky Mountains do not reach high enough elevations that they have a tree line; however, they do sport a number of different tree habitats, containing more than 130 species of trees—more than in all of northern Europe. The 13 national champion trees in the park include the largest sourwood, yellow buckeye, and eastern hemlock. On the park's highest peaks lives a Canadian-type forest of spruce

"Poems are made by fools like me, / But only God can make a tree" wrote poet Joyce Kilmer. The Joyce Kilmer Memorial Forest lies within Nantahala National Forest, where a hemlock (opposite) stretches toward the light within the dark walls of the Cullasaja River Gorge. Riffles (above) make shifting patterns in the Nantahala River.

Resplendent fall colors parade down the slopes of the Bald Mountains. In the middle,

mist hovers over the French Broad River, winding through Cherokee National Forest.

black bears

Behold the bear of the Appalachians. It shambles along, carrying its bulk through forests thick with rhododendron and laurel. The bear feeds throughout the day, perhaps feasting on the sweet fruit of a cherry tree, dining on crickets, ants, beetles, and grubs found in a rotting log, or eating the larvae of yellow jackets nesting in the ground. Although black bears are under increasing threat from habitat loss, the southern Appalachians still support a sizable population. Some 1,800 live in Great Smoky Mountains National Park, with several hundred more inhabiting the surrounding forests.

Bears mate in June and early July; afterward, the male goes off to his solitary existence, with a range of up to 15 square miles. In the fall, bears load up on food. With the onset of winter, they find a good cave or hollow tree and go into hibernation. What happens then makes for good research projects. A few days before the big sleep, the bear eats only roughage; the bear's digestive system forms the roughage into an anal plug up to a foot long that prevents excretion in the den. Cubs are born midwinter, usually two per year; they sometimes nurse for a whole year. One of the fascinating things about hibernation is that while the bear burns up to 4,000 calories a day, he suffers no loss of calcium or bone mass. No other mammal seems to be able to lie still for four months and come out in such good shape.

Preparing to flee to safety, an alert cub clings to a tree trunk.

and fir—nearly three-quarters of all such forest in the southeast. The rich deep soil of hardwood coves favors big yellow poplars, buckeyes, and sugar maples that blaze with color in autumn. Eastern hemlocks grow on cool northern slopes, especially in wet ravines, while pines and oaks take to the craggy, dry southwestern ridges.

Like a separate little kingdom floating high above the surrounding region, this national park is best taken on its own terms. The rich biological mix is due in large part to the heavy rains the Smokies receive—80 inches a year, for example, on Clingmans Dome. Blankets of fog can cover the valleys for long parts of the day. Trails tunnel through dense green forests, and long views are often partially obscured. Some people at first feel closed in. Those who know and love the park treasure its intimate secrets—its wildflower coves, heath balds, rocky streams, and towering trees—knowing that at any moment the veil can lift like magic and reveal the mountain grandeur that is always there, felt if not seen.

The 33-mile Newfound Gap Road bisects the park and travels to several highlights. A spur road leads to the park's highest peak, 6,643-foot Clingmans Dome. A short but steep paved trail makes this high point accessible to just about everybody. Rising in almost the exact middle of the park, the lofty mountain commands exquisite panoramas on clear days. The average visibility has unfortunately been cut in the last 50 years from 93 miles to 22 miles. Ozone pollution has already damaged 30 plant species in the park. Researchers continue to try to improve the air quality. Perhaps one day we can again enjoy the same unimaginably long views seen by visitors in the early 1900s.

Settlers avoided the rugged countryside along the Obed River; they found it unsuitable for farming and too far from the centers of commerce. However, those factors didn't stop the timber industry, which probed into every hidden pocket of Tennessee wilderness in the early 1900s, as did the coal mining industry. Even so, this Cumberland Plateau backwater was so far off the beaten track that when a flood washed out the Nemo railroad bridge in 1929, nobody bothered to rebuild it. Too bad for the town of Nemo, but so much the better for wilderness.

The look of the land can trace its beginnings back some 360 million years ago to when shallow seas covered the area. Compressed layers of sediment became limestone, shale, coal, and sandstone, which were over the course of several millennia uplifted by plate tectonics. Here on the southeast part of the plateau, the layers in some places were heavily buckled into mountains topping 3,500 feet. On the whole, though, the plateau is a rolling tabletop. Rivers and streams were the main sculptors of the topography visible now.

Added to the national park system in 1976, the Obed Wild and Scenic River actually encompasses about 45 miles of four waterways: Obed River, Clear Creek, Daddys Creek, and Emory River. The Obed River accounts for about half of the

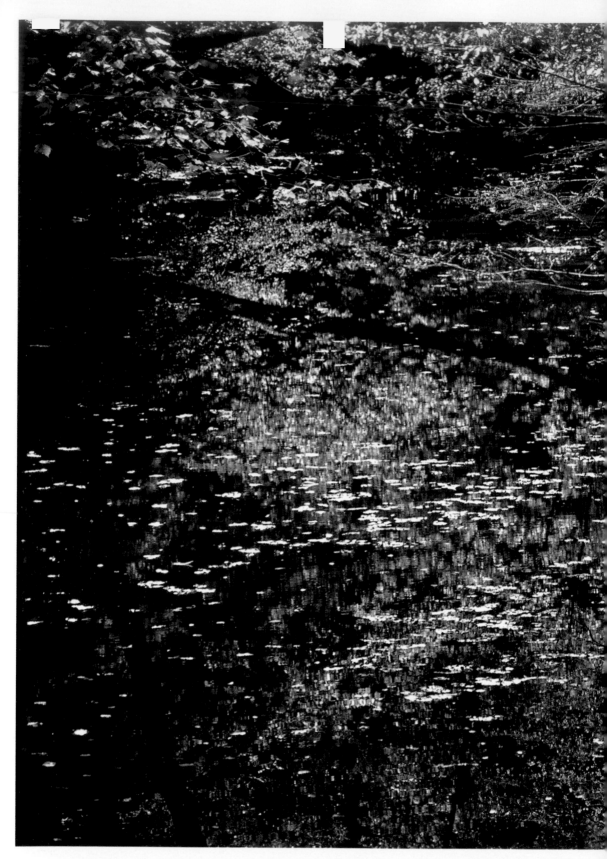

An impressionist painting in shades of green and gold: Autumn leaves reflect

on a backwater of the Big South Fork National River and Recreation Area.

miles in the river park. The streams have gouged out gorges 500 feet deep, lined with magnificent sandstone bluffs; their width, though, creates an effect that is more peaceful than breathtaking—an effect that can sometimes cause inexperienced river runners to discount the "wild" part of the river's wild and scenic designation. Rapids vary from Class II to Class IV, with some of the most exciting paddling on Clear Creek between Lilly Bridge and the creek's junction with the Obed River; just below the junction are some good rapids as well, with names like Canoe Hole and Widow Maker.

But you do not have to be a kayaker to enjoy the river. Plenty of fine swimming holes abound. The one at Nemo Bridge, about six miles southwest of Wartburg, is especially enticing. A rocky beach lines a wide section of the Emory River here, where one can wade in over slippery rocks, then swim. The cooler water lower down feels wonderful on a hot day. Visibility is good enough that, with a mask, one can catch a glimpse of the turtles, big bass, and catfish that make homes here.

The forest across the bridge is composed of second- and third-growth oaks, hickories, beeches, maples, and pines. In cooler, damper areas, hemlocks provide welcome shade, and in the spring azaleas, laurels, and white-flowering rosebay rhododendrons light up the understory with blooms. One mile up from Nemo, at the confluence of the Obed and Emory, you can bushwhack down to a wonderful swimming hole as big as a small lake. Big flat rocks line the riverbank like patios, some of them thin and artfully stacked. I had a great swim here, but afterward discovered that these woods are full of ticks in summer. Seed ticks—larvae of the lone star ticks—are as small as a period, and are devilish to remove. Still, it was worth the trouble for an unmatched piece of riverside tranquility.

An area ransacked for timber and coal in the first half of the 20th century is looking more and more like true wilderness. In the Big South Fork National River and Recreation Area of northeastern Tennessee and southeastern Kentucky, trees, vines, and weeds have grown over old logging roads and are reclaiming mine sites. The history of the mining camps has been preserved in several places in Big South Fork, but in other places there is no visible evidence of man's long tenure here. It is all a big wild landscape of forested bluffs, sandstone arches, high cliffs, and tumbling rivers.

The Clear Fork and New Rivers join to form the Big South Fork of the Cumberland River. North White Oak Creek and other tributaries add their flow to the Big South Fork as it snakes north through the Cumberland Plateau, draining an area of 1,382 square miles. Millions of years ago thick layers of limestone, shale, coal, and sandstone formed. Limestone, the oldest layer, is at the very bottom and is only exposed in a few locations. As the area rose to about 2,000 feet above sea level, rivers began to carve into the land. Since the layers are made of different kinds of rock,

A river otter takes a break in the dappled shade along the banks of the Obed River.

they weather at different rates. This differential erosion over hundreds of thousands of years accounts for the sandstone arches, overhangs, and other fantastic features in the recreation area today.

In addition to its geological wonders, the Big South Fork holds an impressive variety and abundance of wildlife. Black bears from Great Smoky Mountains National Park were released for study in the mid-1990s and are now found in the park.

About 70 percent of the recreation area lies in Tennessee, the rest in Kentucky. Hiking and bridle trails vein the area, many of them old logging roads that dwindle into footpaths. The middle section of the park, the Bandy Creek area, holds some of the most gorgeous and rugged territory, including one of the most impressive natural arch formations in the country. The Twin Arches are two perfectly curved, connected sandstone arches. The combined effect of the two arches together is a powerful reminder of the handiwork of time on a seemingly permanent part of the landscape. Thousands of years from now, the arches will inevitably collapse. All over the area are examples of arches beginning, perfected, or past their prime.

For a bird's-eye perspective of the park, nearby East Rim Overlook offers a dramatic view nearly 500 feet above the river. It also shows why this area is called a plateau: All the river-incised hills are of the same level. It looks as if someone took a giant scraper and flattopped the whole region. Standing here, I tried to imagine, instead, the top of the plateau as the bottom of a sea—which, in fact, it once was. ❧

small gems
of the Smokies

Frozen Head State Park and
Natural Area in eastern Tennessee sticks out like
a sore thumb in winter. The 3,324-foot-high centerpiece of this park rises nearly 2,000 feet
above the valleys, so on cold days the peaks get
coated with ice and snow while the lower lands
stay bare. Frozen Head and other mountains
above 3,000 feet lord it over a stream-lined forest known for its wildflowers and rock shelters.

In the 1890s, convicts from nearby Brushy
Mountain State Prison mined these hills for coal,
and cut timber for the mine props. With the coal
mined out, loggers came and began clearing the
woods. By 1925 just about all the saleable timber
was gone. The forest was beginning to come back
when, in 1952, the area was hit by the worst fire
season ever in Tennessee. Now, more than 50 years
later, the woods are once again lush with oaks,
beeches, yellow poplars, and white pines. Sunlight
sliding through breaks in the canopy gilds ferns
and elaborate spiderwebs.

A maple blazes red in Frozen Head State Park.

Trees find footholds where they can on the sandstone cliffs of Fall Creek Falls State Resort Park.

Fall Creek Falls State Resort Park receives visitors galore, but its ample boundaries leave plenty of elbow room. Here on the western edge of the Cumberland Plateau in east-central Tennessee, streams have opened up huge gorges and left dramatic waterfalls, including the 256-foot namesake falls. The water cascades over a curved wall into a tremendous plunge pool. In winter, the fall freezes into a beautiful ice sculpture with columns and stalactites two stories tall; a chilly spray rimes the nearby vegetation with sleeves of ice.

Along the rim of Cane Creek Gorge are some of the most breathtaking vistas in the state. The roar of wind and water swirls up from 600 feet below. The earliest rock layers, the limestones that were once the shores of a sea, lie at the bottom of the gorge. Up on the bluffs, the younger dark shales and sienna-colored sandstones are burnished gold by the low light of sunset.

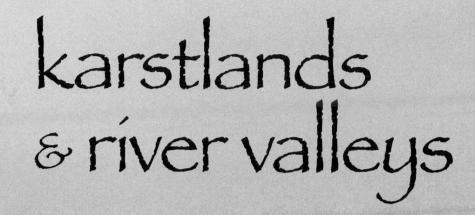

karstlands
& river valleys

"... there is still much to make the heart pound."

Imagine being the first person ever to step into the mouth of Mammoth, or one of the other large caves in the area. What heart-pounding excitement and fear it must have aroused to tread where no one had before, where perhaps man was not even supposed to go. But people did go in—at first for shelter, then deeper and deeper in search of crystals. Later people came into the region looking for a way west, for good land, for coal, for timber, venturing underground for gunpowder material. The virgin forests are gone now, and much of the grassland. We can't know the same sense of wonder and beauty felt by the first people to see Kentucky, but perhaps we can appreciate what's left even more. Underground and above, there is still much to make the heart pound.

Preceding pages: In Cross Creeks National Wildlife Refuge, morning mist rises on a scene of waterside beauty; the refuge hosts over 100,000 migrating waterfowl. Opposite: An eastern redbud leaf hangs ready to fall.

Similar to the Piedmont east of the Appalachians, the land to the west takes its time before smoothing out. In eastern and central Kentucky, the topography is even hillier and more rugged than in the Virginia and Carolina Piedmont. Here spreads a jumbled land of steep gorges, sandstone arches, high pinnacles, and limestone caverns. From the Cumberland Plateau's maze of transverse ridges to the rolling pastures of the Bluegrass to the karst country called the Land of Ten Thousand Sinks, this is the kind of varied region that keeps the eyes constantly busy. And through it all run two key players—the underlying limestone and the rivers that erode it.

Farther west, Kentucky and western Tennessee spread in a low gentle sweep to their borders on the Ohio and Mississippi Rivers. Here streams and rivers that have journeyed for hundreds of miles from the Appalachians drain into the Mississippi, the father of waters. The northernmost reach of the Gulf coastal plain, this area holds pockets of rich alluvial soil, proven by the ubiquitous fields of corn, tobacco, soybeans, and other crops. Of perhaps the greatest interest to nature observers here is the dominating influence of the Mississippi Flyway. Each year millions of ducks, geese, raptors, neotropicals, and other birds migrate along this route, one of the four major north-south flyways on the continent. National wildlife refuges and other preserves give these long-distance flyers a chance to rest, eat, and nest.

To breach the wall of the Alleghenies, early settlers poured through Cumberland Gap, where Kentucky, Virginia, and Tennessee now meet. They learned of the route from fur traders and hunters, who learned it from Indians, who learned it from the buffalo that used the gap to pass into the Kentucky grasslands. No comparable door to the west existed for 400 miles north. Though not the first white men to enter the gap, Daniel Boone and his team of 30 men blazed the Wilderness Trail through it in 1775. Between 1780 and 1810, up to 300,000 people streamed westward on this trail, heading to the rich Kentucky pastures beyond.

Boone's trail eventually became U.S. 25E. The trail-turned-highway once ran straight through the gap; however, in order to restore the gap to its look in pioneer days, U.S. 25E was rerouted through Cumberland Gap Tunnel in 1996. (The tunnel runs between Tennessee and Kentucky; the gap, a half mile north, runs between Virginia and Kentucky.) Cumberland Gap National Historical Park holds 70 miles of trails that explore the fabled gateway. Though the vegetation will take years to fill in, you can now walk through the gap on a piece of the old Wilderness Trail. From nearby Pinnacle Overlook there are spectacular views of the gap and the serpentine ridge of Cumberland Mountain.

Much of the land the settlers first saw is now contained in the Daniel Boone National Forest, running east of the Kentucky Bluegrass region in a narrow 140-mile-long strip from the Tennessee border up nearly to the Ohio border. Within this hilly, rural countryside on the western edge of the Cumberland Plateau are towering

Oaks frame a tobacco curing barn on the edge of Kentucky's Daniel Boone National Forest. Farmland intermingles with the forest's 1,100 square miles.

sandstone bluffs, stream-lashed gorges, mature hardwood forests, and inviting waterfalls. More than 100 species of rare, threatened, or endangered plant and animal life live here, including the Cumberland bean pearlymussel, bald eagle, and gray and Indiana bats.

The forest holds a fraction of the great hardwood forest that once blanketed 75 percent of the state. Logging in the 19th and early 20th centuries cleared out most of the virgin timber, and settlement has kept much of the land open. The forest was in pretty sad shape by the time it was turned over to the government in the 1930s. For decades, the old-growth woodlands had been picked over for the best lumber, the hillsides stripped for iron ore and coal. The soil on this barren, stump-filled landscape washed off, clogging streams and killing fish and other aquatic dwellers. Timber harvesting continues on the national forest, but in a much more controlled way, allowing cut sections to recover. Some coal mining also goes on, though tourism is becoming more and more vital to the area's economy.

Now a healthy mix of young and old forest, the Daniel Boone is filled with towering oaks, hickories, sycamores, and tulip poplars; in spring, before the tall trees fill in with new leaves, the understory redbuds, dogwoods, rhododendrons, and laurels explode in raptures of color and perfume.

Three jewels of the region are found at either end of the national forest. Cumberland Falls State Resort Park is the premier destination in the southern part of

karstlands & river valleys

Pinnacle Overlook in Cumberland Gap National Historical Park offers views of Virginia to the left

and Kentucky to the right. The ridge of Cumberland Mountain snakes off into the distance.

At Natural Bridge State Resort Park, a footbridge (opposite) marks
the beginning of the original 1890s trail up to the famous 65-foot-high
sandstone arch. Massive boulders, some as old as a million years,
litter the trail, sometimes offering hikers a narrow pathway (above).

the forest. The 125-foot-wide waterfall for which the park is named peals over a seven-story ledge with such sudden force that mist forms a constant shimmering cloud downstream and on the nearby trails. On clear nights during or around a full moon, you can see a rare phenomenon called a moonbow—a ghostly light arcing out from the base of the falls. I once drove 40 miles on a twisty mountain road in the dead of night to see the moonbow, and it was worth it.

Natural Bridge State Resort Park in the north end of the Daniel Boone holds 2,250 forested acres surrounding the feature presentation, Natural Bridge. The Original Trail, blazed in the 1890s by the Lexington & Eastern Railroad, ascends through a cool forest of yellow poplar, basswood, sugar maple, and white oak. Pitted and fissured sandstone cliffs line the trail, splotched with lichen in shades of green and orange. At the top stands a massive 65-foot-high Romanesque arch. The 78-foot-long bridge is as wide as a country road—from on top spread wonderful views of the flattopped Cumberland Plateau north and south, gashed with many cliffs and ridges.

Some 150 natural arches exist within a five-mile radius of this point. Natural Bridge may be up to a million years old, while others have formed only recently. They generally begin as a cavelike opening called a rock house or shelter. If the rock house stands on an exposed ridge, the erosive force of wind and rain over thousands of years can whittle out an opening in the soft sandstone, which is capped by a harder, erosion-resistant sandstone. Formations with a small hole are termed lighthouses. As more time goes by, the lighthouse can become a true arch or bridge. Eventually the arch becomes too eroded to support the top, and it collapses.

To the northeast edge of Natural Bridge sprawls the 26,000-acre Red River Gorge Geological Area, a land of arches, sheer cliffs, and stream-etched hills. Some 70 million years of weathering went into the making of this area, the pebbled Corbin sandstone holding on as softer layers eroded away. Cliffs 200 feet high zigzag through the gorge, the iron oxide in the rock giving it a rusty hue. A narrow road follows the boulder-tossed, wild and scenic Red River, and passes through meadows where a score of reintroduced bison graze. The middle section of the river dodges through the gorge. From the top of a 75-foot-long natural span called Sky Bridge, there are superlative views of the gorge.

Tucked in the northern tip of the state along the Ohio River, Big Bone Lick State Park preserves a Pleistocene gathering place for hordes of big mammals. The Pleistocene was a great time for mammals in North America. All manner of creatures thundered, ambled, and trod across the land from 2,500,000 years ago up through the Ice Age. When the glaciers started pushing south about 20,000 years ago, the animals scooted out of the way. The ice made it to just north of the Ohio Valley, where a swampy area with mineral springs looked and tasted awfully good to the animals. Wooly mammoths, mastodons, giant ground sloths, bison, giant stag moose, and primitive horses were among the visitors to these salt- and mineral-rich springs. Mastodons and mammoths (differing from mastodons mainly in their molars) were especially vulnerable in this soupy ground. Many of them got stuck and died. But their bones, covered in the morass, were preserved for thousands of years.

Some 10,000 years ago, the ice retreated and the mammoth disappeared—possibly from overhunting. But a lot of bones had accumulated over the millennia. Explorers began discovering the fossilized bones as far back as 1709; especially noteworthy were the long curving tusks of the mastodon. Some bones collected in the 1760s were sent to Benjamin Franklin, who was so confused by their elephantine nature that he imagined the Earth had been "in another position and the climates differently placed." Thomas Jefferson became so excited by the bones that he charged Lewis and Clark to find out if any prehistoric "monsters" were still living in the West. He, like Franklin and other intellects of the day, had a hard time accepting extinction.

Life-size models give a sense of what the scene may have looked like long ago: A shaggy-haired mammoth stands drinking in a swamp, its stout legs deep in muck. In the low light of early morning or late afternoon, you can almost believe it is real. Elsewhere, a small herd of live (and fenced) bison lends authenticity to the Pleistocene landscape. Trees, grasses, and wildflowers have now filled in what used to be a wide swamp, and the salt-sulphur spring has all but dried up.

Just west of the Bluegrass region lies the Pennyrile, a wooded area of rocky hills and cliffs named for the pennyroyal plant, a kind of mint. The land's many bowl-shaped depressions, some of them hundreds of feet wide, hint at what's going on underneath. Beneath this unassuming countryside of wooded hills, hundreds of caves honeycomb the rock strata, the area's many surface and underground streams having hollowed out tunnels and chambers over millions of years. Including one of the great wonders of the natural world: Mammoth Cave.

With more than 350 miles of known passageways, Mammoth Cave is the most extensive cave system on the planet. And there might be hundreds of miles not yet discovered. But the cave and its spectacularly large chambers are only part of the picture. An interrelated ecosystem combining the underground and the above ground holds creatures as diverse as blindfish and big brown bats, birdfoot violets and freshwater mussels, timber rattlesnakes and great blue herons. For all its treasures, Mammoth Cave National Park has been declared a World Heritage site and the focal point of an international biosphere reserve.

Why did such a colossal work of subterranean architecture end up here? The region happens to have two important cave-making features—layers of soluble limestone underlying a sandstone cap, and plenty of annual rainfall. Hundreds of millions of years ago, a shallow sea covered the region. Countless generations of sea creatures left their calcium carbonate-rich shells to accumulate on the sea floor, packing down

Where mastodons once watered in a swamp, wildflowers now carpet a meadow in Big Bone Lick

State Park. The salt-sulphur spring that attracted the prehistoric beasts has not quite dried up.

A cavernous 20-foot-high overhang on the Cedar Sink Trail is just one of
the many eroded limestone formations within Mammoth Cave National Park.

to create limestone some 500 feet thick. Rivers from the east deposited the sand and
mud that would become sandstone and shale. When the continent rose about 280 million years ago and drained away the sea, the rock layers found themselves above water
level. Enter the rain. Water percolating down through the ground picks up carbon
dioxide to form a weak carbonic acid, which is strong enough to eat away at the limestone. Underground streams formed and constantly probed vulnerable spots in the
limestone, slowly gnawing out tunnels, seeking a way farther and farther down into
the earth. Time was supremely unimportant to the streams—they worked inch by inch
over thousands and thousands of years.

As the water level dropped, higher passages dried out. Then one day about
4,000 years ago, a Late Archaic Indian decided to go deep into the bowels of the
earth. Aboriginals had been living in the area for some 6,000 years, hunting the abundant wildlife and sheltering in the cave's entrances, perhaps exploring a bit. But by
the Archaic period, mineral and crystal collectors were willing to risk their lives, pushing back at least ten miles into the void. Likely the minerals were highly valued for
religious or medical purposes, and were traded with outsiders. By 2,000 years ago,
cave exploration had died out as Indians began practicing agriculture on floodplains
to the west. But footprints, skeletons, and other evidence remain of man's earliest
attempts to plumb the mysteries of Mammoth.

The fields and woods of the park give clues that some extraordinary, unseen
phenomenon lies near at hand. The land is dimpled with sinkholes, some of them

wild turkeys

North America's largest native game bird, the wild turkey is one of the easiest birds to identify. Slightly smaller than domestic turkeys, these strutters have bald heads, the male showing off red wattles and iridescent feathers. They walk along, pausing to peck for seeds, nuts, acorns, and insects, and at night they roost in trees. In springtime you can hear the male gobbling from a mile away.

In 1776, Benjamin Franklin proposed the wild turkey as the symbol of the United States, declaring it "respectable" and "a Bird of Courage." However, since then the bird has fared little better than the bald eagle, the chosen symbol. With habitat destruction and excessive hunting, wild turkeys declined from some 10 million birds in the 19th century to a mere 30,000 by 1950. In 1954 Kentucky's population was estimated at about 850. After many attempts at restoration, mostly by importing turkeys from other states, Kentucky now claims more than 130,000 wild turkeys.

A wild turkey gobbler struts through the forest understory.

Near Mammoth Cave National Park, red maples and cattails stand in Sloan's Crossing Pond,

a body of water that formed in a sandstone depression lying atop the limestone karstlands.

Mammoth Cave is lined with bizarre embellishments that have been created by the deposition of calcium carbonate over thousands of years.

hundreds of feet across, where a cave roof has given way. Tucked into the hillsides are nearly 300 cave openings within the park's boundaries alone. Most of these caves do not connect with the Mammoth system, but all are likely connected indirectly within the area's vast and complex underground hydrology. Imagine a vertical cross section of the park—a tremendous system of leaky pipes, sometimes barely dripping, other times backing up during high river levels.

Mammoth's mapped passageways occur on five levels, down to 360 feet below the ground where an underground river still works at dissolving new spaces. Each level corresponds to a different period in the cave's life, the river having dropped from each level with the force of gravity. Mammoth was gouged out by the powerful force of horizontal streams. As such, the emphasis here is on big architecture instead of precious miniatures. However, the cave has its share of fanciful and dainty dripstone formations. Several rooms in the Frozen Niagara area have exquisite cave decorations: The namesake formation, a 75-foot-high wall of flowstone, appears to cascade from a high ledge. In other areas, stalactites hang like petrified icicles from a wizard's grotto, while cave popcorn, rimstone, and other speleothems bejewel hidden recesses. All these formations are created as water drips through the limestone, dissolving calcium carbonate and depositing it somewhere farther along the stone. Some of the most miraculous gems in the cave are made of gypsum and other minerals, the kind collected by early Indians. The cave also shelters an entire ecosystem of dark-adapted life. Brown bats, eastern pipistrels, cave crickets, blindfish, eyeless crustaceans, and other secretive creatures dwell here, many of them spending their entire lives in total darkness.

Topside, the park offers good chances for spotting wildflowers and wildlife, as well as understanding the connections between cave geology and the surface landscape. The two-mile Mammoth Dome Sink Trail meanders through an open forest of oaks, hickories, and tulip poplars; skirts the edge of a ravine; and then dips into a big bowl-shaped pit. Much of the sink supports small trees and plants, but the funnel, just off the trail to the left, is covered with snags and debris washed downslope. Rainwater can squeeze through the hole and eventually work itself onto the heads of visitors in the Mammoth Dome area of the cave. Farther downhill lies the spring for the River Styx. This river also connects with the cave—a diver could theoretically go down into the pool and emerge somewhere within the cave.

A short way beyond runs the moss-colored Green River, the slow-moving, 100-foot-wide watercourse that winds for 24 miles through the park. Box turtles trundle along the banks; wood ducks and kingfishers patrol the river shoals. Behind rises the limestone-rich hill that contains the cave. Standing here I imagined having x-ray vision—I could turn around and see a hill riddled like an ant farm with cavities and tubes.

Near the park entrance, Sloan's Crossing Pond is a rare body of surface water in this porous land. A depression in the sandstone surface rock has collected enough water to create an entire little ecosystem here. Cattails and arrowroot along the edges hide thrumming frogs; red-winged blackbirds skim the soggy wetlands, looking for mayflies. The life of the pond goes on, oblivious of the world below and of the fact that someday the water will seep away into those mysterious depths and the pond will become a meadow.

Land Between The Lakes, a long peninsula running from Tennessee into Kentucky, sits between Kentucky Lake and Lake Barkley, once much slimmer bodies of water known as the Tennessee River and the Cumberland River. The Kentucky Dam, which forms Kentucky Lake, the largest man-made lake in the East, was built as part of the massive Tennessee Valley Authority project that began harnessing the Tennessee and its drainage basin in the 1930s. Nearly 790 families were forced to relocate when the lake was created; however, the resulting control over the waterways has prevented floods, generated hydroelectric power, and made the Tennessee navigable year-round. After the Cumberland was dammed in 1966, forming Lake Barkley, Land Between The Lakes (LBL) took shape as a 40-mile-long swath of green encompassing 170,000 acres.

Some 300 miles of undeveloped shoreline define the edges of LBL, creating niches for numerous shorebirds and wading birds. Herring, ring-billed, laughing,

In Land Between The Lakes National Recreation Area, native prairie
grasses (opposite) re-create the area's presettlement appearance and
help support populations of bison, elk, wild turkey, and other species.
A monarch butterfly (above) alights on a wildflower along The Trace,
the north-south road through the recreation area.

Awash in light, a deer poses near the Land Between The Lakes Nature Station.

and eight other gull species frequent the area. Great blue herons, swallows, summer ospreys, and occasional white pelicans also take advantage of LBL's wetland habitats. The bald eagle, the celebrity bird species here, makes a good showing in winter, with more than 100 individuals taking up temporary residence. About ten pairs nest in trees in the lakes' inlets.

With habitats ranging from oak-hickory uplands and agricultural fields to lakeshores and bottom wetlands, LBL supports approximately 53 species of mammals, ranging in size from the least shrew to the American bison. The shrew weighs less than an ounce, while the bison, the continent's largest native land animal, can tip the scale at more than a ton. Reintroduced herds of bison and elk occupy a 750-acre preserve in the middle of LBL, while a separate, smaller herd of bison live on two adjacent 100-acre pastures just south. The gated community of elk and bison is one of the highlights of LBL despite the drive-through-zoo feeling. A 3.5-mile road loops a reestablished prairie carpeted by eastern gama, big bluestem, and other native grasses. In summer the shaggy bison wallow in mud or dirt, sometimes right near the road, to ease the torment of biting flies. Elk may prove a bit more elusive, though they are often spotted in the wooded areas between hills.

For a long time, Indians hunted this area, keeping it an open prairie by periodically burning back new growth. By the early 19th century, settlers found the woods beginning to take over and game scarce. Though today's bison cannot thunder across the prairie as their ancestors once did, their presence adds authenticity to the area's look and feel. Up in the sky, red-tailed hawks drift and cry their age-old territorial *scree scree,* while down in the brush bluebirds flash like lapis and white-throated sparrows voice their sweet, plaintive songs.

Kentucky Lake Drive, a short loop near the top of The Trace, a scenic road that runs north-south through LBL, offers time to stop and savor expansive blufftop views of the bulging lake. Herons stalk the shore, gulls wheel out over the water, and white sails glide in the luminous light of late afternoon.

South of LBL, where the Cumberland River begins to swell out to form Lake Barkley reservoir, North and South Cross Creeks add their flow to what still looks and feels like a river. Covering 12 miles of this peaceful body of water, the Cross Creeks National Wildlife Refuge annually welcomes tens of thousands of migrating and wintering waterfowl, and a host of fall and spring songbirds and shorebirds. The refuge's mix of marshes, impounded water, farm fields, and hardwood forest creates a vital habitat for more than 250 species of birds. In fall and winter, the honking and flapping never cease—60,000 ducks of 19 species and 15,000 Canada geese visit the fields and ponds of Cross Creeks to feed and rest.

Threatened bald eagles winter on the refuge, including two pairs that have established permanent homes; endangered least terns sometimes visit. White ibises, sandhill cranes, and merlins are other rare species occasionally seen here, usually in spring or fall. Much more prevalent are wintering mallards, gadwalls, green-winged teals, widgeons, black ducks, and pintails. Among the diving ducks are ring-necked ducks and hooded mergansers. The latter have an especially stylish look, with head crests that, in the male, look like a sleek black fin with a flare of white.

After running through east Tennessee, the long and sinuous Tennessee River dips into Alabama, then turns north and meanders up through west Tennessee. Spaced along the west Tennessee section of the river, the three units of the Tennessee National Wildlife Refuge offer safe haven for up to 350,000 ducks, 30,000 geese, and numerous other kinds of wildlife every year. With about half the refuge's acreage underwater, 40 percent woodlands, and the remainder farmlands, migratory waterfowl find this an ideal place for wintering or resting for flights farther south.

In a cooperative arrangement with the refuge, neighboring farmers leave some of their soybeans, corn, milo, and winter wheat for the birds. In addition, shallow ponds are seasonally flooded to promote the growth of aquatic plants that waterfowl eat. The result is that 23 species of ducks call in here. Though scarce in some parts of the southeast, wood ducks—the ones that look painted with every color of an artist's palette—thrive here, and are the main ducks that nest on the refuge. Ideally they nest in tree cavities, but since it's not always easy to locate a tree with a cavity when you need one, the refuge helps out by providing nesting boxes for this especially beautiful species.

The easiest area to explore by car, even the Big Sandy unit of the refuge takes some map skills to find. I finally did find it on a recent summer trip here, and stopped

Lake Barkley reservoir in the Cross Creeks National Wildlife Refuge is a key

stopover for countless migrating birds coursing up and down the Mississippi Flyway.

at an observation deck off a gravel road that gives onto the Big Sandy River. At this point, just south of its junction with the Tennessee, the river swells to lake size. Great blue herons waded slowly through a sun-spangled sheet of water, while crickets chirped in high grasses and a breeze riffled through the woodlands at river's edge. Though I was here in midday, a ranger told me that in the evening and early morning raccoons and minks hunt along the shore.

At the end of the peninsula that separates the Big Sandy from the Tennessee, Pace Point is a serene spot for spying on herons and egrets posing on a nearby island or along the reedy water's edge. The only sounds here are birdcalls—including the eerie song of the loon—and water lapping the shore. The point acts as a natural funnel for northward migrating birds in spring.

Before 1811, the 20,000-acre body of water called Reelfoot Lake did not exist. In the winter of that year, nature went to work with a vengeance. The middle Mississippi Valley came to life, convulsing and heaving in a series of earthquakes that rank among the most violent ever recorded on the continent. The land all around buckled and split; the ground spewed out hot water, coal, mud, and sulphurous fumes; the river roared as its banks collapsed; waterfowl cried out in terror; and the sky turned black. From December of 1811 to March 1812, three major tremors and hundreds of aftershocks pounded the sparsely populated area. Each of the major quakes was probably higher than magnitude 8, with the greatest estimated at 8.7; for comparison, the San Francisco earthquake of 1906 registered 8.3. The New Madrid earthquakes irrevocably altered the landscape; a huge sunken area in northwestern Tennessee filled with water to become Reelfoot Lake.

The wetland ecosystem created by the lake has been of great benefit to birds and other wildlife. High grasses and ancient bald cypresses that rise on flared trunks fringe the Upper Blue Basin of Reelfoot National Wildlife Refuge. Each season brings new life and energy to the refuge. In the fall, geese, mallards, pintails, buffleheads, and ring-necked ducks flock to the lake in droves, as do some 100 to 200 bald eagles. They winter here, finding the food plentiful and the habitat to their liking. Springtime brings warblers and other songbirds. The hot days of summer showcase resident wildlife: Herons flap noisily to perches in the trees, and summer frogs keep up a steady chorus. The surface of the lake is flat and calm; then a fish jumps, breaking the stillness. Along the water's edge, tiny dragonflies helicopter among the lilies and weeds in brilliant flashes of green and blue, while a party of turtles takes the sun on a nearby log. The lazy pace of the lake in summer gives way in the fall as the skies once again darken with raptors heading south along the Mississippi Flyway. By October chevrons of ducks and geese have begun streaming in, and the life cycle repeats. Just as it does throughout the rest of the karstlands and river valleys. ☙

Fruit of a flowering balloon vine glistens with morning dew at Cross Creeks refuge.

On funnel-shaped trunks, decay-resistant bald cypresses stand at the edge of Reelfoot

Lake. The lake formed during the cataclysmic New Madrid earthquakes of 1811-12.

small gems of the karstlands & river valleys

Metropolis Lake State Nature

Reserve lies hidden near the banks of the Ohio River in western Kentucky. The eponymous lake is one of the state's few remaining natural bodies of water. Bald cypresses, flanked by knobby knees, mirror themselves on the lake's still surface, painting a uniquely Southern scene within hailing distance of Illinois. Red-eared sliders bask along the shore, while kingfishers hover above the water before diving for a catch.

The flared base of a cypress shelters wildlife.

Thick pines frame a flowering dogwood in Bernheim's Big Meadow.

Bernheim Arboretum and Research Forest easily ranks as one of Kentucky's top outdoor beauty spots. This deeply satisfying mix of wildness and horticulture holds scenic high spots from which unfurl long rolling sweeps of green, punctuated by flowering trees and mirror-smooth lakes. The woodlands all around buffer the vast cultivated areas, framing an Edenic landscape that seems almost too perfect to be real.

Among the arboretum's 6,000 labeled varieties of trees, shrubs, and other plants are collections of crab apples, dogwoods, hickories, maples, oaks, and dwarf conifers, as well as one of the most extensive collections of hollies in North America. In all, six different woodland communities stretch across Bernheim. Grasslands peppered with wildflowers are present as well. Important ongoing research projects include stream and wetland restorations.

site addresses

the Coastal Plain

Assateague Island National Seashore
7206 National Seashore Ln.
Berlin, MD 21811
phone 410-641-1443
www.nps.gov/asis

Back Bay National Wildlife Refuge
4005 Sandpiper Rd.
Virginia Beach, VA 23456
phone 757-721-2412
http://backbay.fws.gov

Cape Hatteras National Seashore
1401 National Park Dr.
Manteo, NC 27954
phone 252-473-2111
www.nps.gov/caha

Cape Lookout National Seashore
131 Charles St.
Harkers Island, NC 28531
phone 252-728-2250
www.nps.gov/calo

Chincoteague National Wildlife Refuge
P.O. Box 62
Chincoteague, VA 23336
phone 757-336-6122
http://chinco.fws.gov

**Great Dismal Swamp
National Wildlife Refuge**
3100 Desert Rd.
Suffolk, VA 23439
phone 757-986-3705
http://greatdismalswamp.fws.gov

Jockey's Ridge State Park
P.O. Box 592
Nags Head, NC 27959
phone 252-441-7132
www.jockeysridgestatepark.com

Kiptopeke State Park
3540 Kiptopeke Dr.
Cape Charles, VA 23310
phone 757-331-2267
www.dcr.state.va.us/parks/kiptopek.htm

Lake Waccamaw State Park
1866 State Park Dr.
Lake Waccamaw, NC 28450
phone 910-646-4748
www.ils.unc.edu/parkproject/visit/lawa/
home.html

Merchants Millpond State Park
71 U.S. Hwy. 158E
Gatesville, NC 27938
phone 252-357-1191
www.ils.unc.edu/parkproject/visit/memi/
home.html

Nags Head Woods Preserve
701 W. Ocean Acres Dr.
Kill Devil Hills, NC 27948
phone 252-441-2525
http://nature.org/wherewework/northamer
ica/states/northcarolina/preserves/art5618.ht
ml

Pea Island National Wildlife Refuge
P.O. Box 1969
Manteo, NC 27954
phone 252-473-1131
http://peaisland.fws.gov

the Piedmont

Eno River State Park
6101 Cole Mill Rd.
Durham, NC 27705
phone 919-383-1686
www.ils.unc.edu/parkproject/visit/enri/
home.html

Great Falls Park
George Washington Memorial Pkwy.
c/o Turkey Run Park
McLean, VA 22101
phone 703-285-2965
www.nps.gov/gwmp/grfa

Hanging Rock State Park
P.O. Box 278
Danbury, NC 27016
phone 336-593-8480
www.ils.unc.edu/parkproject/visit/haro/
home.html

James River State Park
Rte. 1, Box 787
Gladstone, VA 24553
phone 434-933-4355
www.dcr.state.va.us/parks/jamesriv.htm

Mason Neck State Park
7301 High Point Rd.
Lorton, VA 22079
phone 703-550-0960
www.dcr.state.va.us/parks/masonnec.htm

Pilot Mountain State Park
1792 Pilot Knob Park Rd.
Pinnacle, NC 27043
phone 336-325-2355
www.ils.unc.edu/parkproject/visit/pimo/
home.html

Prince William Forest Park
18100 Park Headquarters Rd.
Triangle, VA 22172
phone 703-221-7181
www.nps.gov/prwi

Raven Rock State Park
3009 Raven Rock Rd.
Lillington, NC 27546
phone 910-893-4888
www.ils.unc.edu/parkproject/visit/raro/
home.html

Rock Creek Park
3545 Williamsburg Ln., NW
Washington, D.C. 20008
phone 202-895-6070
www.nps.gov/rocr

Theodore Roosevelt Island
George Washington Memorial Pkwy.
c/o Turkey Run Park
McLean, VA 22101
phone 703-289-2500
www.nps.gov/this

the Shenandoah

Buffalo Mountain Natural Area Preserve
Virginia Dept. of Conservation and Recreation
Natural Heritage Program
217 Governor St., 3rd Fl.
Richmond, VA 23219
phone 804-786-7951 or 276-676-5673
www.dcr.state.va.us/dnh/buffalo.htm

Douthat State Park
Rte. 1, Box 212
Millboro, VA 24460
phone 540-862-8100
www.dcr.state.va.us/parks/douthat.htm

**George Washington and
Jefferson National Forests**
5162 Valleypointe Pkwy.
Roanoke, VA 24019
phone 540-265-5100 or 888-265-0019
www.southernregion.fs.fed.us/gwj

Grayson Highlands State Park
829 Grayson Highland Ln.
Mouth of Wilson, VA 24363
phone 276-579-7092
www.dcr.state.va.us/parks/graysonh.htm

Mount Rogers National Recreation Area
3714 Hwy. 16
Marion, VA 24354
phone 276-783-5196 or 800-628-7202
www.southernregion.fs.fed.us/gwj/mr

Mountain Lake Wilderness
New River Valley Ranger District
USDA Forest Service
110 Southpark Dr.
Blacksburg, VA 24060
phone 540-552-4641
www.southernregion.fs.fed.us/gwj/forest/
recreation/wilderness/mountain_lake.shtml

Ramsey's Draft Wilderness Area
Deerfield Ranger District
148 Parkersburg Tpk.
Staunton, VA 24401
phone 540-885-8028
www.southernregion.fs.fed.us/gwj/forest/
recreation/wilderness/ramseys_draft.shtml

Shenandoah National Park
3655 U.S. Hwy. 211E
Luray, VA 22835
phone 540-999-3500
www.npw.gov/shen

the Alleghenies

Babcock State Park
HC 35, Box 150
Clifftop, WV 25831
phone 304-438-3004
www.babcocksp.com

Blackwater Falls State Park
Drawer 490
Davis, WV 26260
phone 304-259-5216
www.blackwaterfalls.com

Canaan Valley National Wildlife Refuge
HC 70, Box 200
Davis, WV 26260
phone 304-866-3858
http://refuges/fws.gov/profiles/index
.cfm?id=51630

Cranberry Glades Botanical Area
District Ranger
USDA Forest Service
932 North Fork Cherry Rd.
Richwood, WV 26261
phone 304-846-2695 (Dec. 1-March 30)
phone 304-653-4826 (April 1-Nov. 30)
www.nps.gov/nero/nnl/cranberryglades.htm

Cranesville Swamp
The Nature Conservancy
723 Kanawha Blvd. E., Ste. 500
Charleston, WV 25301
phone 304-345-4350
http://nature.org/wherewework/northamer
ica/states/maryland/preserves/art135.html

Gauley River National Recreation Area
104 Main St.
P.O. Box 246
Glen Jean, WV 25846
phone 304-465-0508
www.nps.gov/gari

Monongahela National Forest
200 Sycamore St.
Elkins, WV 26241
phone 304-636-1800
www.fs.fed.us/r9/mnf

New River Gorge National River
104 Main St.
P.O. Box 246
Glen Jean, WV 25846
phone 304-465-0508
www.nps.gov/neri

Watoga State Park
HC 82, Box 252
Marlinton, WV 24954
phone 304-799-4087
www.watoga.com

the Smokies

Big South Fork National River
and Recreation Area
4564 Leatherwood Rd.
Oneida, TN 37841
phone 423-569-9778
www.nps.gov/biso

Blue Ridge Parkway
199 Hemphill Knob Rd.
Asheville, NC 28803
phone 828-298-0398
www.nps.gov/blri

Cherokee National Forest
2800 N. Ocoee St.
Cleveland, TN 37312
phone 423-476-9700
www.southernregion.fs.fed.us/cherokee

Fall Creek Falls State Resort Park
Rte. 3
Pikeville, TN 37367
phone 423-881-5298
www.state.tn.us/environment/parks/
parks/FallCreekFalls

Frozen Head State Park
and Natural Area
964 Flat Fork Rd.
Wartburg, TN 37887
phone 423-346-3318
www.state.tn.us/environment/parks/parks/
FrozenHead

Great Smoky Mountains National Park
107 Park Headquarters Rd.
Gatlinburg, TN 37738
phone 423-436-1200
www.nps.gov/grsm

Mount Mitchell State Park
2388 State Hwy. 128
Burnsville, NC 28714
phone 828-675-4611
www.ils.unc.edu/parkproject/visit/momi/
home.html

Nantahala National Forest
Forest Supervisor's Office
160A Zillicoa St.
Asheville, NC 28801
phone 828-257-4200
www.cs.unca.edu/nfsnc

Obed Wild and Scenic River
P.O. Box 429
Wartburg, TN 37887
phone 423-346-6294
www.nps.gov/obed

Pisgah National Forest
Forest Supervisor's Office
160A Zillicoa St.
Asheville, NC 28801
phone 828-257-4200
www.cs.unca.edu/nfsnc

Roan Mountain State Park
1015 Hwy. 143
Roan Mountain, TN 37687
phone 423-772-0190
www.state.tn.us/environment/parks/
parks/RoanMtn

karstlands & river valleys

Bernheim Arboretum and Research Forest
P.O. Box 130
Clermont, KY 40110
phone 502-955-8512
www.bernheim.org

Big Bone Lick State Park
3380 Beaver Rd.
Union, KY 41091
phone 859-384-3522
http://parks.ky.gov/bigbone.htm

Cross Creeks National Wildlife Refuge
643 Wildlife Rd.
Dover, TN 37058
phone 931-232-7477
http://crosscreeks.fws.gov

Cumberland Falls State Resort Park
7351 Hwy. 90
Corbin, KY 40701
phone 606-528-4121
http://parks.ky.gov/cumbfal2.htm

Cumberland Gap
National Historical Park
U.S. 25E South
P.O. Box 1848
Middlesboro, KY 40965
phone 606-248-2817
www.nps.gov/cuga

Daniel Boone National Forest
1700 Bypass Rd.
Winchester, KY 40391
phone 859-745-3100
www.southernregion.fs.fed.us/boone

Land Between The Lakes
National Recreation Area
100 Van Morgan Dr.
Golden Pond, KY 42211
phone 270-924-2000 or 800-525-7077
www.lbl.org

Mammoth Cave National Park
P.O. Box 7
Mammoth Cave, KY 42259
phone 270-758-2181
www.nps.gov/maca

Metropolis Lake State Nature Preserve
Kentucky State Nature Preserves Commis-
sion
801 Schenkel Ln.
Frankfort, KY 40601
phone 502-573-2886
www.naturepreserves.ky.gov/stewardship/
metrolake.htm

Natural Bridge State Resort Park
2135 Natural Bridge Rd.
Slade, KY 40376
phone 606-663-2214
www.state.ky.us/agencies/parks/
natbridg.htm

Reelfoot National Wildlife Refuge
4343 Hwy. 157
Union City, TN 38261
phone 731-538-2481
http://reelfoot.fws.gov

Tennessee National Wildlife Refuge
3006 Dinkins Ln.
Paris, TN 38242
phone 731-642-2091
http://tennesseerefuge.fws.gov

about the author

JOHN M. THOMPSON has authored or contributed to more than a dozen National Geographic books. Giving him a chance to more thoroughly explore the outdoors near his home, *Wildlands of the Upper South* ranks high on his list of all-time favorite assignments. A forthcoming Society publication includes a book on America's Pacific coast. A former resident of Washington, D.C., he now lives in Charlottesville, Virginia.

about the photographer

Freelance photographer RAYMOND GEHMAN specializes in outdoor and natural history subjects. A frequent contributor to NATIONAL GEOGRAPHIC and *Traveler* magazines as well as National Geographic Books, he now lives in central Pennsylvania with his wife and two sons.

suggested additional reading

Berry, Wendell. *The Unforeseen Wilderness: Kentucky's Red River Gorge*. San Francisco: North Point Press, 1991.

Lambert, Darwin. *The Undying Past of Shenandoah National Park*. Boulder: Roberts Rinehart, 1989.

McCague, James. *The Cumberland*. New York: Holt, Rinehart and Winston, 1973.

McPhee, John. *In Suspect Terrain*. New York: Farrar, Straus & Giroux, 1983.

Michener, James. *Chesapeake*. New York: Random House, 1978.

Warner, William W. *Beautiful Swimmers: Watermen, Crabs and the Chesapeake Bay*. Boston: Little, Brown, 1976.

index

Wildlands of the Upper South

By John M. Thompson
Photographs by Raymond Gehman

Published by the National Geographic Society

John M. Fahey, Jr., *President and Chief Executive Officer*
Gilbert M. Grosvenor, *Chairman of the Board*
Nina D. Hoffman, *Executive Vice President*

Prepared by the Book Division

Kevin Mulroy, *Vice President and Editor-in-Chief*
Charles Kogod, *Illustrations Director*
Marianne R. Koszorus, *Design Director*
Barbara Brownell Grogan, *Executive Editor*

Staff for this Book

Jane Sunderland, *Project and Text Editor*
Charles Kogod, *Illustrations Editor*
Cinda Rose, *Art Director*
Peggy Archambault, *Cover Design*
Victoria G. Jones, *Researcher*
Carl Mehler, *Director of Maps*
Sven M. Dolling, *Map Research and Production*
R. Gary Colbert, *Production Director*
Richard S. Wain, *Production Project Manager*
Meredith Wilcox, *Illustrations Assistant*
Dianne Hosmer, *Indexer*

Manufacturing and Quality Control

Christopher A. Liedel, *Chief Financial Officer*
Phillip L. Schlosser, *Managing Director*
John T. Dunn, *Technical Director*
Alan Kerr, *Manager*

One of the world's largest nonprofit scientific and educational organizations, the National Geographic Society was founded in 1888 "for the increase and diffusion of geographic knowledge." Fulfilling this mission, the Society educates and inspires millions every day through its magazines, books, television programs, videos, maps and atlases, research grants, the National Geographic Bee, teacher workshops, and innovative classroom materials. The Society is supported through membership dues, charitable gifts, and income from the sale of its educational products. This support is vital to National Geographic's mission to increase global understanding and promote conservation of our planet through exploration, research, and education.

For more information, please call 1-800-NGS-LINE (647-5463) or write to the following address:

National Geographic Society
1145 17th Street N.W.
Washington, D.C. 20036-4688 U.S.A.

Visit the Society's Web site at www.nationalgeographic.com.

Library of Congress Cataloging-in-Publication Data

Thompson, John M. (John Milliken), 1959-
  Wildlands of the upper South / by John Thompson ; photographs by Raymond Gehman.
     p. cm.
  Includes bibliographical references and index.
  ISBN 0-7922-6893-8
  1. Wildlife refuges--Southern States. 2. Wilderness areas--Southern States. 3. Natural areas--Southern States. 4. Southern States--Geography. 5. Southern States--Description and travel. 6. Southern States--History, Local. I. Title.
  F209.8.T48 2004
  917.5--dc22
              2004007114